Labelled

a Black Villain

Labelled
a Black Villain

TREVOR HERCULES

Fourth Estate · London

First published in Great Britain by
Fourth Estate Limited
113 Westbourne Grove
London W2 4UP

British Library Cataloguing in Publication Data
Hercules, Trevor
    Labelled a black villain
    1. Great Britain. Black persons. Social
    aspects. Black viewpoints. Personal
    observations
    I. Title
    305.8′96′024

    ISBN 0-947795-04-9

Typeset in Plantin by York House Typographic Ltd, London W7
Printed and bound in Great Britain by Richard Clay Ltd, Bungay, Suffolk.

This book is not for sale in the Republic of South Africa.

Preface

I wrote this book because I felt certain things needed to be said, and because those black people in a position to be a real voice for the black community have failed to speak out on our behalf.

The black community still cry out for someone to put forward their real grievances about living in a white society; yet the few black people in a position of power have put across only a diluted version of our anger and frustrations, leaving the white community to go about their daily business without having to confront their conscience head on.

We want society to be in no doubt as to how we as black people – and indeed all third world peoples – feel about the destruction wrought on our lands by the white colonialists of the past and by the economic and political policies of today; and how we feel about the total disrespect shown by white societies for peoples and cultures other than their own.

These things have to be brought out into the open without pulling any punches so both black and white can see where we all stand. We challenge society to a confrontation with its own conscience, to face up to the inequality that divides the world.

At the end of the day, if there is unrest and mass dissatisfaction in the black community, which was and is a feature of American life, let no one say they don't known the reasons.

Secondly it is my wish that we as black people take a closer look at ourselves, and put our lives in order. We have to remember that nothing has to be the way it is. We have to be constructive in our endeavour to improve our lives. With the right state of mind, we can achieve great things. Negativeness will only eat away at our souls, and the good intentions we once had will be eroded – only to be replaced by an empty shell of hate, leaving us disengaged from reality, and sorely disillusioned and embittered.

The Mirror

The ever-presence of paranoia still seems to be with me, pushing me, shoving me, engulfing me with self-doubt.

Times have changed since the early days when an inferiority complex held me tight and would not allow me to step forward. Now I'm forward, I'm back.

Back into the void of suspicion, where I have now become the suspect of a crime that does not exist, paranoia.

In the early days I was ignored, but not now, now they're watching me from everywhere and all the time.

I put my hands in my pockets and hurry by.

Sometimes my head hurts and my vision blurs and I read things into things that are not actually there.

My good friends are deserting me and going over to the other side.

An easier life, they say, where you have more peace of mind. You wear make-up once in a while and when you're told to, you smile.

A smile traded for a consciousness that could have led to an ideal of reality.

Make-up tinged with cowardice to face up to a reality which now hides consciousness.

Run, run, run, run, run. Never too late, never. It's dark, can't see, staggering blindly, I reach out for a hand.

Please help me, I want to see.

Chapter One

As I stood in the middle of the small prison cell I stopped going through my imaginary batting strokes and walked away from my crease which had been marked by a matchstick. I went to the barred window and although it was winter the sun had forced its way through and it caressed my body as my mind drifted away.

'Don't move, get your hands above your head, quick!' We were in now. I held the gun to his head. 'Open the safe,' said Dave as he dragged him towards it. 'I haven't got the keys,' said the terrified jeweller. But we hadn't come this far to be mugged off. 'If the safe isn't open by the time I count to five, you're dead.' He produced a key and began fumbling with the lock but was pushed aside by our youthful impatience. We rifled through the safe, then the shop for choice pieces of jewellery.

We ran to the car, laughing, laughing like two demented lunatics on a high, buzzing without a care in the world. We had the goodies and that was all that mattered. It was the beginning of a life of crime which had now caught up with me as I stood in this small, lonely cell.

I had already been tried and convicted the previous day, for armed robbery, and was now awaiting sentence. I knew I would get a few years but how many I didn't know and I did my level best not to think about it. There had been plenty of activity along the corridor where the cells were situated, and all day people had been going upstairs to the courts and returning downstairs. About fifteen minutes earlier I had heard someone shout out: 'Paul, this is Frank, I got five years.' 'The bastards!' answered the voice.

I only heard the key in the door, but before the screw could open the door I had crossed the cell in two strides and was sitting on the bench with my legs crossed in a very dignified manner. Wouldn't do for screws to see me batting. 'You're next, Hercules,' said a tall screw, as I began walking towards the door where another four screws were waiting to escort me upstairs. They seemed quite polite and began telling me what kind of mood the judge was in and what kind of sentences he had been giving out that day.

At first I was suspicious and thought they might be winding me up, but then I thought they were probably on orders to be cordial because the last thing anybody needs after their freedom has been taken away is some leery screw, so I guessed they must have been picked for their easy-going natures. So I lightened up a bit.

As you can imagine, I had been tense all day – after all, it's not every day that you're up at the Old Bailey awaiting sentence for armed robbery, knowing that the judge is going to send you away for a long time. The walk along the corridor seemed like an eternity and it was as if time had slowed down. Everything seemed so bright that at one point I had to put my hand over my eyes to shield them from the glare. It was like I was in a dream and just floating through it. I was not conscious of moving my arms or legs but I guessed I must have been. They had a life all of their own. I remember feeling this tangy flavour in my mouth, like I had just eaten an orange.

I suppose you could describe these feelings as like being on drugs. Although all these strange sensations were happening to me, I felt really nice and cool and it must have showed because I remember one of the screws saying, 'You don't give a fuck, Hercules, do you?'

'Be lucky son,' said one old boy with his eye pressed to the broken spy-hole of his cell. I couldn't see what he looked like but from his voice I knew he was at least forty.

As we reached the stairs four white guys were coming down with about ten screws. The four guys were making a lot of noise and gesticulating furiously: 'Dirty grass. Fucking slag.' As they passed us one of the screws was talking about them, but the only thing I really heard was that they were a firm from the East End charged with about ten counts of armed robbery; I vaguely remembered them being in the papers some weeks ago. I suppose they looked like stereotype villains, if there is such a thing, suited up with hard faces that showed a hard life – expensive gear that somehow would seem more fitting to men of a much softer and gentler appearance.

By now we had arrived at the top of the stairs and were into a spacious area with doors about every twenty yards, which I assumed to be the doors leading into the different courts. The area was a hive of activity; how people knew what they were doing was beyond me.

The screw who was leading our party stopped suddenly and, looking perplexed, began to look around him – the idiot was obviously lost. I say idiot because he had a piece of paper with instructions that he had been following since they had fetched me from my cell. 'It's court number four,' said the screw with a grunt. We proceeded to court four.

All through my life I had hated the system, fought against it and tried to do as much damage as I could. To think they were about to sentence me, me rebel, warrior, Kitindo. *You bastards, I don't believe in your system or your judgment. I don't recognise you or your system, we should be trying you for your sins, you bastards, you destroy everything you touch with your hands of death. Oh how I hate you.*

I am a political prisoner. I am a prisoner of war, you bastards, I justify myself because you stole our wealth, our gold, our diamonds, our bodies, in fact you stole our birthrights – I hate you and will never give up the struggle, never.

It had happened again – my mind slipping into that light area of consciousness, that area that made me an extremely angry young man, angry at the things I saw in the world, yet which at the same time gave me an air of tranquillity and great insight into myself as a man: a human being, carrying the torch of light, the torch of awareness, awareness of myself as a black man that gave me the confidence and guidance to be proud yet humble, to be loving yet cold, to be placid yet violent, yet also to hold no fear.

The slipping into the light had become more frequent over the last months, but always with it came the anger, that unmoving anger, that intolerant anger. The anger knew it was right, and because it knew that I agreed it came more and more to the front, urging me to stand up for my rights, to stand up for my black identity, because it could never be free until my identity had been freed.

The mental anguish and frustration at knowing you've been wronged, the one-man crusade, the people who understand your grievances but refuse to help, saying, 'What can we do?' – was all part of the anguish and frustration that added fuel to my anger.

From the dock I surveyed the splendid scene in front of me. I say splendid because Hollywood couldn't have stage-managed a better setting. I stood in the dock right at the back of the court. The dock was raised about three feet off the ground, surrounded by panelling about crutch-height when standing; a long bench was inside so when you sat the panelling was about chest-height. Two screws stood on either side of me in the dock, and about four stood around the dock with their heads just below the panelling. Straight in front of me at the other end of the court sat the judge. His platform was higher than mine by about a foot and a half, and the distance between us must have been at least twenty feet. The inevitable half-moon glasses were perched on the end of his nose and his immaculate white wig seemed to be just an extension of the judge himself. I got the feeling that if he took off the wig he would die, and for some reason that wig seemed to be the most important thing in the court. Then a flash of inspiration came to me – it was not Regina the Queen who was the power, it was that nasty wig, kill the wig and you kill the system – I was a genius.

In front and below me were rows of pulpits – that's the only way I can describe them, because it seemed that everyone there were on their knees, praying to this wig, their God. They were like a mixture of black-caped draculas with wigs, and pin-striped businessmen telling the boss that they had sold more products than Braithwaite, and their sales figures had doubled for that year.

The dreamlike state I had been in had gradually subsided.

The prosecution lawyer was up now, standing with legs together, hands outstretched as he listed my previous convictions, every so often turning to me as he spoke the words 'assault' 'offensive weapon', then flicking his fingers with a flourish in my direction as if to say, 'That piece of shit!' The man had centre-stage, and he loved every minute of it. It was his stage, his domain, his territory and he knew today would be an easy day: a working-class youth in the dock, ignorant of the élite's ways, already found guilty, and the icing on the cake was that he was black. *Everyone knows black youths are criminals*, he might have said.

'I say, old boy, I was found guilty of assault which I did NOT commit, I'm just the victim of a miscarriage of justice.' He glared up at me in the dock with scorn, which for a minute looked like real scorn. It wouldn't be such an easy day after all.

'Keep quiet, young man, you'll have your chance,' said the wig.

When I had seen my solicitors previously they had tried to go through my mitigation with me – mitigation being really a begging speech, saying why you did it . . . I have a dying mother, I needed the money for my grandmother's heart transplant, that kind of thing. Saying that my mother had left the family and I had been in homes most of my life would be true, but was too much like begging for me, so I told my solicitor that no way, under no circumstances did I want them to make a plea of mitigation on my behalf. And I certainly would not. I had already made myself clear to my counsel (the barrister or 'brief' representing me in court) that no way would I submit to the shame of begging this court and bringing my family life into it so that they could judge my family as well. That was *my* instruction to *my* counsel and I had him promise that he would abide by it. Now, right in front of me here was my brief, the dirty liar, talking about me coming from a broken home, and how my mother had put me in care from an early age.

'Shut up your dirty mouth.'

By this time the court was in uproar.

'I sack you. I don't want this man. I sack him, I represent myself from now on.' By now myself and several screws were struggling in the docks. 'Get off me, you bastards, you whores!'

I was removed down the stairs of the dock and outside into the spacious area where one of the doors, surprise, surprise, turned out to be a cell. I was left for about fifteen minutes to cool off.

I was born in this country and speak English very well, but when I wanted to dissociate myself from this society I lapsed into patois. I was deeply ashamed of the fact that I had been in children's homes most of my life, and the fact that my mother and father had split up, with my mother putting me and my younger brother in a home, while leaving my father to care for my brother and two sisters. I hated my mother, or so I believed, yet I could never forget that warm smiling face and the warmth of her bosom and smothering kisses when, as a family, we had been together. I hated her the many nights I lay in bed in those children's homes and cried myself to sleep. At times it hurt me so bad inside when I bullied my younger brother even to the point of hitting and making him cry, so he could be tough enough to look after himself without crying when other people hit him. Worst of all, I hated my mother for the way she had left my younger brother who was about five or six – it was all right for me at ten, but my brother cried constantly and I had to make him cry even more so he knew it was just the two of us and no one else. I hated her for the way she had abandoned us to other people to do what they would with us. Of course, I didn't believe in God. Hadn't I asked God a million times to help me and my brother and not once did he even acknowledge me – which is strange because all the homes we were in were Catholic homes, with priests and nuns running around everywhere.

I hated my mother for letting a young warrior who could have changed the world or been what he wanted to be suffer the shame of being unwanted, because even as a child you feel the lack of respect towards you, and you become very sensitive. Perhaps that's why in some respects I'm very cold now; but then again so are most people who have spent large parts of their lives in homes or institutions. There's no love there – just hardness.

For as long as I can remember, social workers, child-care officers and probation officers have tried to talk to me about my mother and family in general, but not a word would pass my lips even though they had the basic facts: that my mother had left myself and brother in a home and gone to America. I suppose they had to try and find out what I felt about it just because they could never get anything out of me. One of the reasons why I would never say anything about my family or discuss my mother was that I clung to the hope that in time everything would once again be all right and our whole family would be together. I had visions of my mother appearing with an explanation. Mind you, it would have had to be a good one – you know, something like that she had been mentally ill but doctors had cured her – then I would have been able to forgive her and we could all live as one. I always believed my mother would have a good explanation because secretly I loved my mother very dearly; or rather, subconsciously I loved my mother dearly.

I had some very vivid dreams of one of the priests or nuns calling me into their office and telling me to take a seat, then making tea and telling me my mother had been found wandering around the streets with some mental illness, and had been taken to hospital and would be coming out soon to collect me and my brother John. And the part that always made me the happiest was when they said, 'Oh, and by the way, she sends her love.'

So you can see that I didn't really want anyone to judge my mother, least of all people who didn't know her, people who made a living from assassinating people's characters. I certainly wasn't going to let them rip my mother's character apart and judge what kind of a mother she was. If anybody was to do it, it would be me and my family, and only us. Imagine my horror when my brief began telling the court that my mother had abandoned her family. He might as well have been telling the whole world. I just flipped.

The door of the cell opened and standing in the doorway with several screws was the young lady who took notes for my solicitor on the occasions he had interviewed me. She now stood apprehensively at the cell door trying to look very cool, but with that look that black people know so well – that mixture of fear with a need to explore the unknown, frightened by all the old racial crap that a black man is an animal, black man is violent, black man lusts after white woman's body. She was in a male-dominated cocoon, with the burly screws surrounding her, to protect her, her white knights in shining armour, and with her adrenalin running high she faced this black masculine animal, this black stallion. She was being used as women have been used throughout history, sent by her masters to come and tame the raging black bull.

'I'm sorry, Trevor, I told him not to read it out,' she said in her best little girl's voice. 'I'm very, very sorry, Trevor.' I just looked at her in the fashion white people often used to call truculent, but which we as black people know is the look of being pissed off. 'It's okay.' She smiled, mission completed and successful. She could now report back to her masters. 'We're going into court now, Trevor, I'll see you later.' She turned and left.

I was back in the dock again and the anger that had previously boosted me and kept me strong had now left me. I looked around the court for assistance but there was none, not even a friendly face, no black man to look at, to relate to.

Then it hit me: I knew why there were no black faces in the court, they were all in the cells below, hundreds of them, millions of black faces locked in the cells, locked up in all the prisons in England. I was a genius. I began to giggle. Everybody looked up at me but no one said a word. The court was very quiet now and the only sound was the judge rustling some papers around on his bench. My heart began to beat faster, my legs to feel very heavy – I had difficulty in breathing, a rushing sound came to my ears and that glare came back to my eyes, the funny taste returned to my mouth. It had all happened as suddenly as that. This was it, it was time, the moment of truth. The court was hushed as the judge began to speak.

'You, Mr Hercules, have been found guilty of a very serious crime. You are obviously a danger and menace to our society, therefore, by the power of this court, I hereby sentence you to seven years imprisonment.'

The previous night, in my cell at Brixton Remand Centre,

I had been rehearsing all these revolutionary speeches I would deliver from the dock after I had been sentenced – you know, things like: 'You may lock me up but you'll never lock up my mind, the black struggle will continue and we'll destroy your system.' But I must admit that when the judge sentenced me I was stunned, I was truly shocked. I just managed to get my black-power salute in before I was hustled out of the dock and down the stairs and marched back to the cells.

The years of being in children's homes plus the life I had been living prior to my arrest had helped me to condition my mind so that I could switch off and remain impassive to a lot of things that I didn't really wish to deal with. I was able just to accept it without letting it get to me, a kind of cold acceptance of the situation – like it was all happening to someone else and not me. But later, during my sentence, I was to realise what seven years of imprisonment really meant and this realisation left me shell-shocked. It took me a long time to come to terms with it.

The reason that I had been put in a single cell earlier on, before I came up to be sentenced, was that I had told a screw to fuck off when he said, 'Hello sunshine.' But now they put me back in a very large cell with the rest of the convicted prisoners. The cell they had put us in was about three times the size of a normal single, but even so it was crowded. About thirty men were inside in various forms of array. There were those who had been lucky enough to get a place on the bench, but for the rest it was a back-to-the-wall job, some sitting with hands on their knees while others just leant on the walls. Even though there was some conversation between the prisoners, it couldn't hide the resigned dejection and apprehension of what lay in store for us all. We were just like cattle that had been herded together in the pen to be slaughtered. We were there for that purpose and that purpose only – regardless of who you were or where you came from, you were the same as the next man in the cell. This was a different society. In here we would make our own moralistic judgments and our own punishments, and in time we would have our own hierarchy, whether we liked it or not. There was nowhere to run, no escape, nowhere to hide. To survive in this environment, I needed to be very strong both physically and mentally. And I promised myself that I would be.

I surveyed my fellow prisoners and the sight was not pretty. I suppose you have heard the expression 'motley crew'; well, they were right here. My God, I'd found them – perhaps I should let someone know. Having said that, they, or rather we, all had something in common, as most prisoners everywhere in the world do. From my assessment we all seemed to come from working-class backgrounds. We were the products of high-rise concrete jungles with the stench and the piss and the lurid graffiti that covers the walls, and the rows of streets with cars at least ten years old and mostly broken down, some being supported by bricks because someone had nicked the wheels; the products of the rising ghettos and all the evils they gave birth to; the products of a society where daily confrontations with the police are considered normal; the products of a society where jobs are hard to get, and a job that has any intelligence or pride attached to it is even harder. We were people who knew about prison even before we reached it, because probably at least one member of the extended family had had a prison experience. We were people who had dropped out of school or been expelled and didn't care anyway, because the classrooms were over-crowded, the teachers overworked and not really interested as long as they got through the day – besides, who wanted to learn the rubbish they taught in schools about Napoleon, or where Saigon was on the bloody map. We were people who needed to be shown how to get jobs or fill out our unemployment cards and our milk tokens. We were people who needed to be shown that even though we lived in ghettos there was a way out, and not just through crime. We were people who had seen our parents work and struggle throughout their lives with nothing to show for it, that's if we knew who our parents were. Men who live with violence or the threat of violence, make no mistake, become very hard men.

We were the products of a capitalist society where profit is the order of the day – capitalism as defined by the dictionary: dominance of private owners of capital and production for profit.

And here we were assembled together because of our common pursuit of that goal, *wealth*, by the only means we knew how. We wanted some of the goodies: nice big cars, expensive clothes, nice big houses.

After all, hadn't the media put it across to all of us who lived in our cocoon of ignorance that, in order to be macho and to get the most beautiful girls, we needed the latest-model car, the dream kitchen, the trendiest furniture, the yacht by the sea, the holidays abroad. That was what we wanted, some of the good life. Then our families and friends would really respect us. 'John is doing quite well for himself, you know, lovely car, big house, and you want to see the new kitchen he's bought for his wife. Oh, did you see the diamond ring he bought her, God yes. It must have cost him a fortune. Mind you, God knows how he does it, but then again, who cares? Good luck to the fellow.'

But it's all a dream, a dirty lie, and all of us were here to prove it. The prisoners all over the country and all over the world proved it, proved it conclusively as far as I was concerned. It was a lie. Because the quest for wealth, this elusive wealth that only a minority got, was a carrot for us, the needy, so we chased and chased the carrot until our whole lives were taken up with a quest which consumed us. We slept, ate and drank wealth. Wealth was our goal. Our God. Those who had the wealth were not about to share it with anyone else, least of all yobs from a working-class background, and they had their henchmen, the police, to see to it.

When I had entered the cell several people had acknow-ledged me, with nods of 'All right, mate'. Some of the people I knew through being on remand together, some I did not know. Prison etiquette meant I was left alone for some time to collect my thoughts. They now obviously thought that I'd had enough time to reflect because someone was asking me how long I got. 'Seven years,' I muttered. I had taken up position against the wall by the door where I could survey the room without turning my head. 'What did you get nicked for?' 'Robbery,' I replied. The same guy had asked me the previous question and it seemed that he had elected himself spokesman. I guessed he must have come from Wandsworth Remand Centre, as he hadn't arrived on the bus from Brixton with us earlier in the morning. He was probably about six foot with very broad shoulders and a thick black beard, but the most striking feature was his very blue piercing eyes. He sat with three of his friends who I learned had all been charged together, with robbery. They were all expensively and tastefully dressed.

Soon I had found myself in conversation with two other black guys from Peckham who had been charged with conspiracy to rob. And of course the conversation turned to women. They insisted that South London girls were the prettiest while I held strong in favour of West London, and Harlesden in particular because I knew some very lovely ladies in Harlesden.

The conversation was cut short by a screw calling out our names – I say short but we had been locked up for three hours. We were on our way. The usual mode of transport is what is called a 'sweat-box'; you've probably seen them driving around the streets but it's hardly likely you would know what they are really like. They are a cross between a police horsebox and an armoured van. The best way to describe the inside is if you imagine sitting on a dining-room chair and then putting a box over yourself and the chair without any room to move backwards or forwards or sideways and just about two foot above your head. Now let someone cut a hole in the outer side, about seven inches by five and at face height. Then you come close to realising what a sweat-box is, and believe me, you sweat. As I said, that was the usual way of transportation, but today we were travelling in green Transit vans with bars on the windows. We were handcuffed in twos and led out to the vans.

I would now have to go to Wormwood Scrubs Prison to be allocated to a long-term maximum-security prison. It was nearly Christmas, decorations were everywhere and the lights had been turned on in Oxford Street; the place was alive with colour. I had seven years to do; seven years of my life would be gone. I wouldn't see next Christmas, or the next, or the next, or the next. God. I felt depressed. I thought about my friends and what they would be doing: they would definitely have a draw (weed) and enough drink. I began to hate everybody and blamed everyone for my present predicament. What would happen to my clothes? Would they fit me when I eventually came out, would they still be in fashion? Where would I live, where would I get money, who would employ me, would I still be able to have sex?

All these things ran through my mind on that unforgettable journey. I remember the van feeling cold as I hunched myself up against the window, one hand in my pocket while the other was in the middle of the seat cuffed to some white guy. Even though my cuffed arm ached I didn't say anything to the guy because I just didn't want to talk; so when he moved his arm around a bit, I just moved my arm with him. It was cold, yet I would have given anything to have been outside in that cold, chilly night, that wonderful fresh, chilly night. I imagined the prison officers coming up to me and saying things like, 'If you take off all your clothes and walk home we'll let you go' or , 'If you hop all the way home you can go.' Sometimes the conditions were really hard – like no sex for a year, that was a hard one – but to every offer I said 'Yes.' I was desperate to get out of this van. I even thought about escape, but that was not on. The door was secured by several locks with one screw sitting at the front of the van carrying the keys while several more screws sat at the back and sides of the van. Besides, where was I going to go, me a black man with a white man attached to him like some kind of monkey.

I turned to the window and began to think about how much I hated this country, and the people in it. I say I hated the people, but that wasn't strictly true. I really admired Bill Logey and thought a great deal of him, and he was white. Bill Logey had been my child-care officer off and on during the time I had been in care and I had nothing but respect and admiration for that man, because he had proved to me that although he was white, he was a humanitarian, and lived his life accordingly. Anything that he didn't like or thought was wrong, he spoke up against it. I remembered one summer being with Mr Logey at the child-care office in Holland Park. Mr Logey was in an office with one of his superiors, having an argument about me. Being only twelve and quite nosy, I glued my ear to the door to listen. From what I could make out, Mr Logey's superior was trying to move me from the home I was in to some really horrible place, but Mr Logey stated quite firmly that it was out of order and that he would be making a complaint higher up about the way that this particular home was being used as a dumping ground for all the black kids who they as child-care officers found difficult to deal with and on no account should I be placed there. I'm glad to say that Mr Logey got his way.

What I hated most was the idea of white supremacy, the way the world was governed by a minority of white people who controlled the world with their economic and political power. I realised that it was a racial struggle for us black people to emerge out of this shadow of white supremacy and to be able to live as we chose, without this society continuing to label us as blacks and a problem. I also realised it was also a class struggle, too, and the months I had been in prison on remand had made this even clearer to me. I didn't hate white people individually, I hated how they allowed this powerful minority to oppress and manipulate them, and to turn man against man, brother against brother, just on account of the colour of a man's skin.

Three years ago, at the age of seventeen, I had discovered black writers. They opened up a whole new world to me and within their pages I found my identity, I found myself and with it an understanding of my experiences in this country. Most of the black writers I had discovered were Americans but that didn't detract from the importance of what they had to say, in fact it enhanced it. It brought home the similarity of being black in America and being black in Britain. It was really a wonderful experience to be able to read all these books that I could relate to and identify with, and I could often be seen with my head buried in books in the oddest places, the loo being no exception as many people will testify. It had been great reading white writers with their white characters, such as Ian Fleming and his 007 hero, but no matter how much I tried picturing myself as James Bond it always seemed a bit strange. Nothing could compare with the joy of finding writers like James Baldwin with their black characters sharing their experiences with us, enduring the same things we went through. Then we had people like Eldridge Cleaver, Angela Davies, Rap Brown, Malcolm X; and then Bobby Seale with *Sieze the Time*, the most influential book that I have ever read. These people began to lay a foundation of my awareness of who I was, my identity as a black man. They talked of Africa, they talked of the black man's history and the social and political implications of being black in capitalist societies; they helped me become articulate in explaining the problem facing black people.

In America at the time they were going through a very

tense and political struggle over unemployment, bad hous-
ing, ghettos, crime, police brutality, racial murders – all in a
society that was riddled with racial prejudice, a capitalist
country just like Britain. How our struggle came about may
have been different, but the feelings and experiences were
the same. Their struggle in America evolved from slavery;
now they were an embarrassment to America, a problem just
as we black people were in Britain. They had been cast off
into ghettos at the bottom of the economic scale with not
much hope or future in a society which had no respect for
them and discriminated against them because they were
black. While we here in Britain suffered a similar but much
subtler form of discrimination. Their experiences helped me
put the struggle of black people in Britain into a clearer
perspective. I was now able to reason logically, politically
and socially quite well. Words like 'socio-economic' came
into my vocabulary! Racism, prejudice, colonialism, imperialism, nationalism were topics I discussed with friends, and
as time went on I became ever more politically aware. I
began to find out how other countries were run and what
political systems they used, how they worked and their
results.

When I found black history books, or rather found history
books written by black historians, it blew my mind. What
was this I read, black people had great civilisations? I had to
read on. Then I was so astounded by this revelation that I
ran as fast as I could to different museums to find out if I
could confirm it. I was slightly dubious. I mean, I had never
been told black people had a great historic past. The only
thing my school history had taught me was that black people
were slaves, always dependent on the white man; and this was
a constant thorn in my side. At school the minute they talked
about black people it was time to get hot and slide down in
your seat hoping nobody would look at you, damning and
cursing every black man that ever lived for making you feel
so ashamed. Another thing: if black people had these great

civilisations, surely they would have taught us about them in school. So when up popped these black historians making these wondrous claims, of course I was a bit doubtful. But inside I was alive, I was on fire, my heart jumping, to think this might actually be true. Deep down I had always believed black people must have made some form of contribution, but the revelations were far beyond my wildest dreams.

The new-found pride I felt after discovering these claims to be true was there for everyone to see. I would ever so casually start conversations with friends, then just throw in the names of great black kings and queens. It didn't matter what the topic was, you could have just said 'Hello', and I would still find a way to get a conversation going about some ancient figure in black history. But it seemed that most black people didn't know their history, so usually I ended up telling people about the wonders of past African civilisations.

With all this new-found knowledge came a pride and dignity that gave me a feeling of walking on air, and any feelings of inferiority had been replaced by one of superiority, whether rightly or wrongly, about my people's civilisations. The Egyptians were black people, and they founded one of the earliest and greatest civilisations of mankind. It was the early seventies, and I was bubbling.

But then came the anger, the anger at the white race who had conspired to hide my history from me, who had lied about the way slavery really was and had set out to destroy black people's credibility. The respect I had for their historians disappeared overnight: they were liars, racists, scum who connived to rob me of my heritage. They were lying schoolteachers who said black people were not so badly treated as slaves, lying historians who told me South Africans sold their land to the Europeans – how could I have believed such a lie? I hated the churches who said love your brother yet would not stand up and denounce the policies of South Africa. Why did the Church not stand up and tell every christian who came to church or believed in God to denounce the apartheid system, where men were considered inferior because they were black? I denounced the Church and all the Catholic upbringing I'd had; after all, hadn't the Church played a large part in slavery and colonialism? They went to Africa, gun in one hand and bible in the other – they were just a bunch of Bible-pushing hypocrites. As Bob Marley said, I felt like bombing a church now that I knew the preacher was lying. I hated the politicians who appeared on television saying how there was a 'black problem', and they were doing all they could to solve it, while at the same time they were pushing us into ghetto slums, implementing racist bills to screw us down even further, exploiting Africa's resources and manipulating the West Indian economic and political scene like skilled puppeteers. I hated the white race for being fooled into believing we were their enemies. While we were fighting, black against white, the politicians and their rich, blue-blooded friends were reaping all the rewards and getting fatter and fatter. I hated the police who were hired by these gangsters to carry out their dirty work. The experiences suffered at the hands of these bully boys confirmed to me and the rest of the black community that we had a formidable foe.

Although the anger was strong, I had mellowed from the confused sixteen-year-old who would lash out at the slightest provocation, and had become very reluctant to fight with black guys, whom I had now progressed to calling brothers as they did in the States. I was now making allowances for black people's behaviour because there was a definite relationship between violence and the black community – a relationship born of frustration at their miserable existence. Rather than fight I would try and explain that as brothers we shouldn't fight each other but the system that kept us oppressed. This, in fact, gained me a lot of respect among the black community – especially because they knew I was not afraid to fight, as the nickname 'Mad Dog' which I was given suggests.

We had now arrived at the Scrubs. The driver bibbed his horn and the gates of hell swung open.

Chapter Two

Entering the gates of Wormwood Scrubs prison on a cold December night was just like entering Dracula's castle. Once inside, the van drove through a maze of arches, the driver feeling his way through the darkness. I couldn't really believe this was actually happening to me as we pulled up outside a door with an iron gate and four screws with dogs surrounded the van. This couldn't be England, I kept thinking to myself, surely they had made some mistake, this was Alcatraz or some other such horrific American prison I had seen portrayed on television.

They herded us into a large, brightly-lit room which had a long bench against the far wall that was able to seat all of us; a curved counter stood opposite the bench with about three screws behind it checking the files of prisoners and delegating orders to trustee prisoners (prisoners who were given red armbands as a sign of their trustworthiness. These prisoners made tea for the screws and in general could best be described as screw's runners.)

I had been in Brixton Remand Centre since May and it was now December. While the atmosphere there had not been cordial, it was nothing compared to the atmosphere this place generated. There was a feeling of electric tension that stared straight at me. I guessed the rest of the prisoners must have felt it because there was little talking. But then we were going into the unknown, because it was the first time most of us had experienced being convicted and sent to jail. As I surveyed the scene I saw that there was one important reason for the electric vibes: the screws were altogether different from the ones we had experienced before – not that they were bigger, but their attitude seemed to be much harder. They appeared cold and distant and they didn't attempt any form of conversation; there was a barrier between them and us. And the way they talked to the trustees left us in no doubt as to their attitude to us as prisoners.

They had that cold, blank-eyed stare of zombies, that stare you usually associate with a complete lack of interest or sympathy, and a hardness that came with dealing with hard men. I thought how easy it would have been for them to reverse roles and become prisoners. By now the screws at the desk had begun to call us up one by one to be stripped of our own clothes and issued with prison clothing, and a prison number. We were stripped of all personal possessions, even cigarettes were taken, also chains and rings; you were left with nothing that personalised you. We were now prisoners of Her Majesty's Government. We were given the same uniformal dress – blue-striped shirts and black shoes with blue jeans and, most important of all, your prison number. You were no more a name but a number. There were hundreds of Smiths or Cartwrights but there was only one person with your number, and that was you. As we talked among ourselves, we all agreed that this place was dread. Our prison sentence had now truly begun.

The process of being stripped naked and having your possessions taken from you was bad enough, but the attitude of the screws on the desk was inhuman; any question you asked was nearly always met with 'Because I said so,' or 'You are just a prisoner.' There was never any explanation and you had to accept that. The smirking screws with peaked caps and highly-polished boots who stood around with arms folded didn't give you any incentive to argue – you got the impression they were doing their best to dehumanise you. Any defect you had, they would use against you: 'Hey you, fatso,' or 'You with the rubber lips, get up here.' They were conditioning you to accept that you were nobody, with no one to help you, and any feelings of pride you had were now strictly taboo.

'What's your name?'

'Hercules.'

'How long did you get?'

'Seven years.'

The screw at the desk was looking at my file. I had already promised myself that I would try to start off on the right foot and get out of prison as soon as possible and with the least fuss. I vowed to let any remark pass that wasn't too bad, but the screw at the desk had other ideas as he weighed me up, and I him.

I showed no fear of him as our eyes met, and he knew it. The way I carried myself upright and proud was bound to be a point of confrontation. I wanted to look down at the ground when he stared at me to show my submissiveness, but I was unable to and that age-old confrontation between white man and black man came into play. Now it was not just the matter of me being a prisoner, it was a matter of me being a black prisoner who was proud and non-subservient to white men. He threw down the challenge and I accepted, even though I didn't want to. The challenge was in the way we looked into each other's eyes and we both knew that the collision was inevitable. He was confident in his position as a screw with the help of the system to back him up; I was confident with the knowledge of the people I had left behind on freedom street, confident that they would like me to conduct myself with pride as a black man, a black man who represented them even though they were not here to see me. I was confident in the fact that I would not let my family down, or my ancestors who had to bear the indignity of slavery. I was representing the black race. I was young, arrogant and proud – and to see me you would know that – unafraid of any physical challenge that had to be met. I wouldn't look for trouble but I wouldn't run. Even if I wanted to hide the fact, I could not. I was a product of a life lived with violence, as were others from the cesspools of urban slums like the one I came from, Ladbroke Grove. I had an aura of violence, it was in the way I walked, talked, looked. My friends and I had bad reputations for not standing for any crap – many a time we'd pulled guns on other little firms, and fighting people with knives was commonplace. We were hard young men, though later on I was to discover I was a very nice young man compared to the evilness of some whom prison had made very bitter.

'Pass over those pictures,' said the screw, his eyes laughingly daring me not to.

I passed them over. 'When will I get the pictures of my girlfriend back?'

'Shut the fuck up, Rastas.' I hate being called Rastas.

I smiled, picked up the pictures of my girl and ripped them up as we stared at each other. 'Fuck off.'

He smiled. This had been what he had been waiting for, and I was later to discover that this was a favourite pastime of screws – baiting black prisoners so they could take away their remission.

I heard a distant bell ringing and the sound of footsteps as blue-clad figures overwhelmed me. Who were these people? Police? For a minute I had lost my bearings. No, they were screws. They hustled me away to the block which they call the segregation unit, pushing and dragging me along the way. You know those movies on television where you see someone put in a padded cell and they don't see anyone, except when their meal is brought? Well, the segregation unit is something like that.

The cell was dark and I sat in a corner hugging my knees. I hadn't been beaten up or anything but I was badly shaken. Beneath my hard exterior was a lonely unsure youth of twenty years old in a situation that was alien to him. New territory and boundaries would have to be crossed during this prison experience. I would have to learn in here, mature with time, because this would be my life for the next seven years. I didn't have anyone to help me. I was on my own and they could do what they liked – I must do my best to remember that. As I sat in that dungeon-like cell I thought what it must have been like during those times of slavery and I remembered that on several occasions on freedom street I had stated that I would never have been a slave, and that those who were enslaved should have taken their own lives. Such statements now seemed shallow and rash, the anger of a young man ashamed that his people had been enslaved, frustrated at the way black people were still enslaved in South Africa, and economically, racially and politically oppressed all over the world. The conclusion I came to that night was that it was possible for any race to be enslaved, but the true worth of the people was to be prepared to die for their freedom.

I woke the following morning feeling a lot less cocky – no wonder the place is also called 'the cooler'. My body ached and I realised I'd have to tread a bit more carefully; these people didn't mess around. I could just about lie down on the floor with my feet against the wall and hands outstretched, which gives you a fair idea of the length and width of the cell. The bed was six inches off the ground and instead of springs it had three- inch strips of iron up and down the bed to support the mattress, which was a piece of three-inch foam with a large hole in the middle; I guessed a previous inmate had made it, in every sense of the word! A chair and desk were the only other pieces of furniture. A small plastic chamber pot (commonly know as a 'piss-pot') stood in the corner, and a white plastic jug stood in a blue plastic bowl.

The door opened and a screw stood in the doorway reading some nonsense about me from a piece of official-looking paper. Roughly translated he said, 'You, Trevor Hercules, have been charged with section something under paragraph so and so, and you did commit this above offence at approximately ten pm at the main reception area.'

I couldn't believe he was serious and I looked at his face for some kind of sign that this was a joke. There was none. I had been charged with abusive language and would be seeing the prison governor some time that morning, when I would be able to state my case.

Later that morning four screws escorted me, still in the segregation unit, to a door which we waited outside patiently. There was another entrance to the room four feet further along the corridor. It was out of this other door that a screw with as many medals as a US Army general appeared. He had medals, ribbons and stars on his chest, his cap, his sleeve, and for all I knew or cared he could have had them on his underwear as well. Just as I was wondering how he kept them all clean, or whether he got his wife to polish them for him every day before he came on duty, he ordered the screw in charge of running the block to take me in.

I was brought in and told to stand on a small mat. Four screws stood around me, very close. The two in front and facing me were nearly touching me physically, while the other two stood behind me. In front of me were some waist-high railings, behind which sat the governor, with his henchmen standing beside him. The screw who I had told to fuck off the previous night was also there.

'Name and number to the governor,' said medallion man.

'Hercules, but I've forgotten my number.'

He then proceeded to tell my my number and not to forget it in future. They began to read out the charge with all sections and paragraphs, etc. I was asked if I understood and if I did, what did I plead, guilty or not guilty? As I was about to answer, the screw to the right and facing me poked his tongue out at me and begun pulling all these funny faces. Of course I started laughing, at the same time telling him to pack it in. Here was this big overgrown screw with a moustache like Jimmy Edwards pulling all these funny faces which his colleagues behind me could obviously see, though they said nothing.

The governor was furious. 'Take out the prisoner, and bring him back when he is not in such a jolly mood,' he shouted.

'But governor, this man was making me laugh by pulling faces.'

They were now hustling me out of the door while I went on trying to protest to the governor.

I was taken back to my cell, where a screw told me it was time to get my dinner. On a trolley outside my door were two plastic plates with what looked like food on them. The plates had hundreds of scratches on them that had turned brown, probably with dirt. I wondered where they had got them, and if they had been washed, and if they had, who had washed them. The potatoes were a muddy colour and the slice of meat on the plate looked like dry cow shit. The two screws who were pushing the trolley looked at me in that funny way people who don't like you look, and I felt that if I did take one of the plates they would close the door as quickly as possible and say: 'My God, he is going to *eat it.* Personally I couldn't believe that anybody would really touch the stuff. There is one thing I don't mess about with, and that is my food. I was now very vexed, especially as I knew there would be no more food forthcoming. I said, 'I don't want any.'

The screw didn't say anything but went to close the door; my foot was there first, stopping the door from being closed. 'Excuse me, please, shouldn't I be on the wing with the rest of the prisoners?'

The screw looked at me and smiled resignedly, he had seen it all before. 'Oh, didn't they tell you, Hercules? The governor has given you seven days solitary confinement with seven days loss of earnings. You will be with us for seven days.'

With that he started to squeeze my foot in the door. I decided to move my foot – he looked a bit big, but the real reason I did so was the way he was smiling as he squeezed my foot in the door. That smile was definitely not normal. I sat down on the chair and began to think how it could be possible for a man to have so much power as to take seven days of my life away without me being present and without me even being found guilty.

A prison segregation unit, fondly referred to as the 'block' or 'cooler', is usually annexed from the main wing. It is like a prison within a prison, but a prison for punishment, whichever way you look at it. It usually has about ten cells and a 'strong box' (padded cell). The block has its own rules and regulations and as far as I know nobody knows them, so that means you can break them at any time without knowing it. The only time that you do know you've broken one of the rules is when a screw appears at your cell door first thing in the morning brandishing a charge sheet, telling you that you have been placed on report and what for. The routine is very strict and they do their best to make it as unpleasant and unbearable as possible for you so you don't want to come back. After all, this is the system's form of control, or one of them, for men whom they regard as unruly.

The cells usually face each other about ten feet apart, then there is an office for the screws and, usually opposite that, a toilet for the inmates, which consists of one or two urinal bowls and a toilet to sit on. I say toilet to sit on, but crouch on would be more appropriate because no prison toilet I have ever seen had a seat that could be lifted up or put down. Instead of a proper seat each side of the top of the bowl has a piece of wood about six inches long screwed into it for you to sit on – very uncomfortable. The door of the toilet is only a half a door, as many prison toilet doors are, so that your upper body can be seen by anyone passing, which means you can never have a crap without everyone knowing who is stinking up the place. It is very embarrassing. Ask anybody who's been away, one of the most pleasurable things about being released is a crap in peace without people watching you and telling you to hurry up. Inside, no sooner have you sat down on the toilet then someone is saying, 'Haven't you finished crapping yet, Trevor? Hurry up, man, you've been in there five minutes.' It's very embarrassing, as I said.

The routine of the segregation unit at the Scrubs wasn't too different from any other unit around the country. About seven o'clock the screws come on duty – you always knew when they came on because of the jangle of their keys as they walked, which told you it was time to get up. There were usually five or six screws allocated to the block and around seven-fifteen they started slopping out the prisoners. I know we were prisoners, supposedly paying for crimes we had committed against society and all that, but we were still human beings who had to go back out into society. Nevertheless, every morning, regardless of whether you were in segregation or on the main wing, when the screws opened your door in the morning they bawled 'Slop-out!' like you were some kind of animal. Slopping-out consists of empty-ing your piss-pot, because after seven o'clock at night you cannot get out to use the toilet and even during the day it is up to the screw on duty to use his discretion – which means that it depends on who it is and what kind of mood he's in. So many things in prison depend on the whim of the screw in charge. You get water for washing your plates and face and, if you can find one, a broom to clean the cell. You are allowed two trips to the recess. In the segregation unit you are not allowed to see anyone else who is in the unit, so that means they only let one man out at a time. Your brother or cousin could be in the cell next door and you wouldn't see him. The block was a very lonely place to be.

Next, at about a quarter to eight came breakfast, when two screws and an inmate not on punishment came round with a trolley with food. About nine o'clock we slopped out again to clean our plates and throw away dirty water, or any other such chore we had. Depending on the whim of the screw in charge, we either went on exercise in the morning or the afternoon. If the morning looked bad they left us until the afternoon, hoping that the weather would get worse so they wouldn't have to take us out at all. They did that especially in the winter, because they had to stand up in the cold for an hour as we walked around. Like most prison segregations units, the block at Wormwood Scrubs is largely self-contained and has its own facilities, including a small, square exercise yard. You got the feeling that if a bomb was to hit the main prison building the block would still be functioning. Exercise consisted of walking clockwise around the square, which at times could make you quite dizzy. You were not allowed to go anti-clockwise, run, sit down, or talk to anyone who passed. All these things were an offence and as well as your exercise being terminated if you violated any of these *unwritten rules*, you could also be placed on report.

It may seem really irreverent, but the meeting place in prison is church, and on Sundays you can see the church filled with prisoners. It is used as a meeting place because in every prison they have more than one wing and prisoners from one wing are not allowed to mix with prisoners from another – and moreover you don't even know *who* is on the other wings. So everybody goes to church in the hope of a joyful reunion with some long-lost friend. Whispering to your friend about ten benches away usually makes Sunday church-going quite an event, and it rarely ends without trouble for someone. Usually that trouble comes in the form of screws taking someone away, or in many cases dragging them away.

I had been brought up from the block by two screws and we had taken up position at the back of the church on the right-hand side. I assumed I was the only one from the block because the only screws from the block sat with me. The block screws always sat with the people on punishment – it made them feel good to be looking after the troublemakers. Their whole posture would change, their chests would inflate and they would keep coming up to you on some pretext to whisper some rubbish in your ear. They made a big thing of getting you a hymn book and at the end, when it was time to leave, they would wait until a few rows of inmates had started departing before stepping in dramatically and halting the flow of traffic to make a big show of ushering you out in a Sweeney-style operation. As the priest was halfway through his sermon, two tall black guys were being brought in by about four four block screws. I was told to move up and the two new arrivals were given seats beside me. I'm fairly tall at five feet eleven, but these guys were at least six feet one, but it wasn't because they were big and tall that I knew they were special people. They had that confident air, that aura that surrounds a proud person. They sat down, looked at me, smiled and nodded. That smile and nod represented something, because in jail you keep yourself to yourself and check someone and see what calibre of man they are before you entertain them. They were black brothers and they had clearly acknowledged me as the same – not just a man with a black skin, but a true brother. I was conscious and aware and so were they. There was a feeling of comradeship. Though we could have probably got one or two words in before the screws stopped us, we said nothing to each other; there was no need for words. They both had on patches, thick yellow stripes down the sides of their trousers and on the back of their jackets, to show that they were prisoners who had attempted to escape and were under special watch at all times.

The service was now over, and the four screws ushered

out these two prisoners before anyone else could move – but not before another exchange of nods.

The days in the block really dragged. It was lonely just looking at four bloody walls day in and day out for twenty-three hours a day. I didn't have any tobacco and I hadn't had any since I came into the block and I was dying for a roll-up. I had already searched the cell floor for dog-ends. Thank God I hadn't found any, because it's anyone's guess what I would have done. Every time I left my cell to slop out my eyes were glued to the floor all the way to the recess and back again, but I never saw one dog-end and I remained without a smoke. Then, on the fourth day of punishment in the block, a piece of paper was pushed under my door by the red band cleaner. It read, SNOUT BEHIND THE TOILET, RING THE BELL. I finally persuaded the screw to let me use the toilet and, lo and behold, behind the toilet bowl on the floor was a brown envelope. Sitting on the bowl with my eyes still ahead, I just reached down until my hands found the envelope and then quickly pocketed it. The reason I had to retrieve it that way was to ensure the screw didn't see me, which he could have done easily through the half door of the toilet.

I sat down on the chair and opened the envelope like a crazed junky looking for a fix. To my joy I found a lump of tobacco, cigarette papers, matches and a piece of strike. In my haste to build one up, I nearly missed the note inside: ENJOY YOUR SMOKE, I'M OFF TO MAIDSTONE TOMORROW, JEFF.

Jeff was a friend I knew from outside and we had had a lot of fun together and I felt a bit sad that I didn't know where or when I would see him again. It made me unhappy to think that most of the people I grew up with were inside – or if not inside, getting ready to come inside, because they too were rebelling in their own way against a system and society that had alienated them to the point where they didn't want to be any part of it. Some were people whom I knew to be good, who would give you their last penny and help others at the cost of their own freedom, people without whom the black community would be nothing. These were the people at the front line of the action who didn't stand for shit. They made it possible for black people to walk the streets unmolested because they let everyone know black man would fight back, black man would stand up for his rights. These same black people were the real heroes of the community, and if not for them, the rest of the black community would still be slaves. 'Right on, brothers!' I shouted at the top of my voice. 'Keep the noise down, Hercules,' said the screw, his eye poking at me through the spy-hole.

Released from the block on a Friday, I arrived at the office of the main wing with my prison gear stuffed in a pillow case over my shoulder. The screw who had brought me from the block popped his head into the office and said 'One on, Sir,' and left. The wing was a hive of activity as people were coming down for their dinner. The steel trays that dinner was served on had different compartments – one for dinner, one for soup and another for the sweet and they always seemed to be banging and clattering against the body or some other object. The screws keys were no better – jangle, jangle, jangle, everywhere you turned. I thought maybe my sensitivity was due to the fact that I had just come out of the block where there was hardly any noise. In a way the familiar sounds were comforting me with the knowledge that at last I'd be able to speak to people again.

'Have you got your cell card with you, Hercules?'

'Yes.'

I handed the screw my cell card, which was a small card kept outside your cell with your name, prison number and cell number. This was one of the authorities' strongest security measures because it meant they could check you out any time, anywhere. With so many men about they couldn't know everyone, so if they caught a few of you in a cell they would ask your name and number and if it didn't correspond with the ones on the card outside the cell, you were in trouble.

The screw wrote my new cell number on the card. 'What religion are you?'

'Not that I don't believe in God, but as far as . . . '

'I didn't ask you for your life history,' he interrupted.

I shrugged my shoulders. 'None.'

'You have been allocated to Cell Three, could you take him up, Sir,' he said to a screw who was sitting down and who looked like he had just gone the full fifteen rounds with Joe Frazier with only his face for protection – I was later to learn he fancied himself as a fighter.

Even though I was in jail, I didn't feel too bad or too isolated, mainly because there were a lot of black prisoners and as black people we tend to live in communities. Nearly all of us knew someone personally or indirectly through someone else and, like any minority, we tended to stick together because we had a lot in common. As I climbed the stairs to my cell I was greeted by a lot of inmates, some who had been with me on the first day, some who had earlier been at Brixton, and others who just greeted me because they knew I was coming from the block.

As the people greeted me I just nodded my head with a smile. It was like they were paying me my due respect and I suppose I enjoyed it like some real celebrity. 'Hail, dread.'

'Chevor.' 'Roots.' 'Lion.' 'Rude boy.' These were some of the things the black prisoners were shouting out, and I was also greeted by a few white guys who knew me. 'All right, mate.' 'Nice one, son.' 'Sweet.' The cell I was allocated was worse than a pigsty. At first I wanted to blame the guys, but then on reflection I realised that it must be nearly impossible to keep a cell clean that is shared by three men who at any time could be shipped out. There was barely any room to move, our clothes were changed once every week and we had a bath once a week. One sheet and your pillow-case were changed weekly, but the blankets were never changed.

When I looked at my two blankets I can honestly tell you they were the dirtiest blankets I have ever come across. I had to use them after about the second night because it was so cold, but I told the landing screws that it was impossible to sleep with such filth. They said if I couldn't find any better ones in an empty cell then I'd have to make do with the ones I had. Because the prison was full and there were no empty cells I had to use them, sperm stains and all.

The two guys I had to share the cell with were white. One was in for armed robbery, the other for some petty charge and didn't have long to serve. Tony, who was serving four years for robbery, I'm sure was a lunatic and should not have been in the Scrubs but some nut-house. Many a time I'd hold a conversation with him and he'd say something and I would have to look at him to see if he was serious. One night we were talking about robbery and I was telling him about how years ago I had robbed a rent collector who from my information source should have had five grand, but only had one and a half. We took it and let him go. Tony got excited and started to bounce up and down on the top of the bunk-bed we shared.

'No, no,' he said. 'No, you should have held him and tortured him.'

'Why? He didn't have any more money, we searched him thoroughly.'

'That is not the point, is it?' said Tony. 'I always carry a bit of string in my pocket and when I get them I tie the string around their balls and squeeze it tight.'

I thought he was going to say that he would have done this to find out whether the man had more money, but when I asked him he said, 'So they never forget me.'

I said, 'They wouldn't know you anyway, Tony.'

'Oh yes, they would,' he said, 'the man with the string who tied up people's balls, they'd remember him all right, the shit cunts, I hate them all, Trevor.'

I still don't know who he meant when he said he hated

them all, but I promised myself I was going to get a move out of this cell the next day.

I moved in with two other black guys who had asked a white guy in their cell to swop with me. He said he would because apparently he didn't like sharing the cell with two black guys, and my friend Bevan laughingly told me how the guy never slept, as if he feared they might do something to him during the night. As far as they could gather he didn't know much about black people and was very wary of them. Every morning the guy was a wreck from lack of sleep and so he gladly accepted the change. He had yet to meet Tony!

Prisoners are sent to the Scrubs to wait for allocation to a long-term prison. Every day people would be told what prisons they had been allocated to and then they would await the weekly or monthly buses to those prisons. About two weeks after I moved cells, a white guy, another Tony, whom I knew from Brixton was asked by the PE teacher to get some people together for a football game in the yard, and he came and called me – he'd been let out of his cell to collect recruits. 'Hey, Trevor, want a game of football mate?' he said banging on my door. 'Yeh, man, put my name down immediately.' I also asked him to put Bevan's name down, which he did, as nearly everyone wanted to play to break up the monotony and boredom of being locked up all day. After dinner those who had been chosen to play were unlocked and congregated downstairs, but Bevan and I had been kept locked up despite our energetic bell-ringing and door-banging. You have a push button embedded in the wall and when this is pushed it rings a bell and throws out a black flap outside the door that signals your cell number, so any prison officer standing at one end of the landing can instantly hear and see who has rung their bell. Every time our bell flap went down someone walked by and put it back up again, but when we asked who it was we never got a reply. We knew it was a screw because there was no mistaking that familiar jangle of keys.

By now we had missed the football and we just sat down in our cells and we cursed everyone, but most of all we cursed white man, as we as black people seemed to do whenever we congregated because we saw them as the cause of our oppression. That is true enough, but the continuing resentment towards white man was not very constructive and often led to feelings of bitterness within us. When we spoke of hatred for white man we really meant those in positions of power, those who manipulated society. When we were finally unlocked for slop-out, Tony came up to me. He came from North London and he knew just about everyone there was to know in the criminal underworld and was regarded as one of your own, a real staunch guy. Although he was thick-set and had the look of boxer, he was really very gentle and kind, but if it came to a row he would steam in all right. 'Sorry, mate, I told the screw you were down on the football list, Trevor, and he said he was going to unlock you. I didn't realise he hadn't unlocked you until we were out of the gate and then I called him through the bars, I said, 'have you let Hercules and McGrow out of their cells?' He just looked at me and smiled – the rat – dirty no good dog, I thought the geezer was having a laugh, Trevor, it was a right liberty.'

By now several guys had crowded round me and Tony, some who had been playing football and others who were just taking an interest. We were in the recess where there is a big enamel sink called a sloosh where you empty your piss-pots, and which has two taps to wash plates and get your drinking water. It serves at least seventy men so you can imagine the stench with men living on top of one another and being locked up all day. Any distraction from that tedious boring routine of everyday prison life came as a welcome change, so even if they didn't actually join in the discussion about why some screw didn't open someone's cell door, they took their time slopping-out so they could at least listen. A few people made comments like 'animals, shit-cunts, vermin'. Even Bevan kept saying over and over,

'Nastiness'. These remarks were made about screws in general and not directed at any one screw in particular. Although there were several screws scattered about, they didn't take much notice because it wasn't a disturbance – we were still slopping-out and talking at the same time, only a bit slower. By the look of things Bevan and I were the only black guys who had been picked to play, because certain black guys were now asking me and Bevan what was going on. We were explaining when a black guy asked which screw it was, which was a good idea because Tony hadn't actually pointed him out. When Tony described him, I and everybody else knew that it was none other than Joe Frazier's sparring partner, the screw whom I had first met on leaving the block but who was now apparently off-duty. Bevan and I and a few others went down to collect our tea, still discussing the incident. We knew it was a waste of time to see the principal officer in charge of the wing, but we asked him how it was that my cell was not unlocked. The principal officer's own words were, 'tough'. We didn't say anything, we just left; by now we had quite a delegation discussing this screw, and the general consensus was, he was a dog, or as Nyah put it, 'a batty-man'.

It was seven o'clock next morning and the cell door was opened by Frazier's sparring partner. 'Slop-out time.' He poked his head into the cell, smiled, looked around and said, 'Good morning, boys,' before moving on to unlock the next cell in line. We were all in a state of semi-dress but the three of us stopped what we were doing and stared at the empty door-frame. We knew we were being baited but what could we do? Not only was the screw very big, but we were in prison and didn't have any rights. At the touch of one of the buttons that were placed all over the wings many men in blue would come running with big sticks to cool us down. They also had padded cells and straitjackets for people who disturbed their peace, but the biggest threat was of the governor taking days, weeks or months of your life away through loss of remission.

We hadn't had time to say anything before he had gone, and we all still felt bad in our own way. I honestly believed I should have run after him and had a go, and I felt even worse in the knowledge that this screw, who by his record and actions we knew to be a racialist, had added insult to injury by challenging our pride and daring us to have a go. Then he could show his might and power with the back-up of his army of blue men, who supposedly stood for law and order and justice – they were the good guys, we were the bad guys, criminals. He was onto a good form of entertainment, baiting black guys. He couldn't lose, because he had the system on his side.

These things flashed through my mind as I completed dressing. I thanked God that my friend Dave wasn't around to see what to me and him constituted behaving like a negro, not standing up for your rights. We as men had endeavoured to be proud, especially in the face of racial hostilities. We weren't no niggers for no man to take advantage of or liberties with. A man called you black bastard or wog, you didn't ask questions you just steamed in. Even as far back as school I can remember many a time we fought back to back against guys and never flinched, even in confrontations with our dreaded enemy the police; yet here I was having the piss taken out of me by some screw. What could I do? At least fighting police outside you had a chance to get away, but here you had no chance, there was nowhere to go.

The boxer stood outside the recess with two of his buddies sharing some secret joke that seemed to be funny. I walked straight past them and into the recess. 'Good morning, Trevor,' the boxer said. No screw calls you by your first name or says good morning, that much I'd learnt, but the way he said it, '*good* morning, Trevor' emphasising the 'good', had his companions smirking like someone had a finger up their asses. I didn't bat an eye but carried on what I was doing, ignoring him and his friends completely, as if I hadn't heard him. The other inmates in the recess knew what was happening and you could see people hanging around looking for some excitement, but I wasn't going to oblige them or the boxer and his cronies – not just yet, anyway.

Dinner time came and went without any incident and after dinner was canteen. That is when you are allowed to spend your wages, which is about 80p – or enough to get you half an ounce of tobacco, matches and Rizla. Bevan was on a visit and the other guy in the cell was seeing the welfare office so I brought half an ounce, promising myself I would give up so as to be able to buy orange juice, sugar, or some other luxury. After purchasing your canteen you are supposed to go back to your cell, but most people find an excuse to go to the recess to talk and smoke with friends whom ordinarily you wouldn't see, apart from at exercise time. In the recess I joined a few prisoners, including my friend Nyah, and we got into a deep conversation about Rasta when someone said a screw was coming and people started to disperse. He came right towards myself and Nyah, ignoring everybody else. 'Why are you not in your cells?' the boxer said, looking at me and Nyah. Nyah who was in front began to give him some elaborate tale of how he came to be there. While he did I just looked at the boxer. Not saying a word he stood there, like some slave-master putting the fear of God into his slaves, demanding an explanation while other white prisoners walked off without a word being said to them. It could be any story so long as we showed sufficient subservient fawning.

'What about you, Hercules, what is your excuse?'

I stared at him, it didn't occur to him that I could or would be anything but compliant.

'Fuck you, your mother and sisters are whores and you suck cock.'

Even though I hadn't said it loudly the people in the near

vicinity heard it. After all, they were expecting some form of confrontation between myself and the boxer and were waiting for the outcome. The boxer smiled and said, 'All right, everybody back to your cells,' and with that he moved off in the direction of the canteen. As we went back to our cells people congratulated me on my bravado for telling him like it was: 'that's good enough for him, the slag, about time someone told him.' But I found it was mostly the white guys who were were saying these things, and as I walked towards my cell with Nyah and two other guys, they were shaking their heads and saying to me that I was very stupid.

'Don't you know that is what he wanted you to say, Trevor? He doesn't care what you call him because he's immune to insults. Most of these screws are or else they couldn't spend their lives locking and unlocking cell doors. Now they're gonna take away some of your remission for nothing. Before you came he was fucking with black people, he's put the most black people in the block and not a day passes by and he doesn't have some bust-up with a black man. Don't follow those white guys who like all that excitement, let them be the ones to tell him, they are the villains. Just laugh at him, Trevor, he's pathetic, don't let him get to you, don't bring yourself down to his level'.

As I began to explain why I thought what I did was right, Bevan came charging up the stairs: 'What's up?' he said. 'Did you do him? It's about time we all go and mash him up; the man's been taking pure liberties with black man for too long.' He turned to me and grabbed my hand and said, 'Nice, brother.' Thats why I like this guy, he doesn't let no man take liberties with him, he stands firm.

Because we had so much time to talk being locked up, Bevan and I and our cell-mate had got into some heavy discussions on black awareness and our cultural history and I, being quite knowledgeable or well read, had influenced Bevan quite considerably. Most evenings we could be found lying on our beds talking about great African civilisations, which my cell-mates seemed not to know much about but were eager to listen to. They were fascinated by accounts of the proud Zulu and Ashanti empires, and by this time my friend Bevan had taken to calling everyone brother and telling people to be proud of their black skin and stand up for their rights. He had promised to look me up when we were released so we could take a trip to Africa. I loved the man as a real brother.

The procedure for being placed on report was the same in all prisons. If an inmate committed an offence, they didn't actually take him to the block the instant the offence was committed, because this could sometimes lead to a rebellion by the rest of the inmates; so what happened was that before anyone unlocked in the morning your door would open with three screws outside and they would tell you that you were on report. This meant that at times you didn't know whether you were on report or not until your door was opened early in the morning and you were told to pack your toothbrush, sheets, pillow-case and any letters that had been sent to you. So they came for me the next morning, and obviously I had been expecting it. I don't know if it had been planned or what, but I got the same cell that I had been in when I first came into the block.

I had two letters that had been sent to me by a dear sister who I had been having a relationship with before I had been arrested, and as I came into the block I was told I had to be searched. I loathed being searched, it made me so angry to have a man running his hands over my body; sometimes it was more of a caress, it was degrading. The letters I had from my woman were in my hand and one of the screws said he had to look at them to see what was in them. I refused and they told me that they had their jobs to do. Even though they were the only thing that I had that made me feel warm and kept me human, I knew I had to tear them up. They were like a part of me, precious papers that if I gave over to the enemy, I would be considered a traitor. I tore them up in little pieces in front of the screw. 'That's your prerogative,' said the screw, as I was left in the cell alone.

The meeting with the governor was the same as the last time: I gave my name and number and explained to the governor the boxer's record of placing black people on report and his general racist way of baiting black people. The governor got mad at the suggestion that one of his officers could be racist and told me that since I had been in his prison I had done nothing but cause trouble, and for my trouble he was giving me seven days segregation and seven days loss of earnings.

To help my loneliness and frustration at being locked up I developed some amazing games to play, and took off into fantasies that would have been good enough for any movie screen. I was now becoming conditioned to being on my own. I had time to think and act out some of my fantasies, much to my embarrassment at times. Once I was Bob Marley and was giving a concert in Lagos, Nigeria. I was introducing my band and as I began to play with all the Bob Marley mannerisms, the eye from the spy-hole asked if I needed the doctor, to which I replied with my favourite 'Fuck off'!. Then there was the time I was fighting for the heavyweight crown of the world, stripped naked except for a pair of underpants. I had the killer on the ropes and was talking to him while pounding his ribs, only for the eye in the spy-hole to say, 'Leave it out, he's dead now, champ.' At times I really felt sorry for myself, especially when it got dark during the afternoons with the overhanging clouds and everything in the cell so dull, drab and grey. At those times I could have sworn I was in hell, without a friend in the world. I was on my own and felt I knew what it must be like to be marooned.

Chapter Three

As we waited to go into the visiting room we stood on a kind of shoe-box to be searched; we were searched before and after visits. I entered the visiting room and felt confident. The visitors' brightly-coloured clothing was like a field of brightly-coloured flowers by contrast with the shabby prison wear.

There was no mistaking Dolly and as I walked towards the table where she sat I thought she was the most beautiful girl not only in the room, but in the world. She was here to see me and I felt like a king as the other black guys turned around in their seats to catch a glimpse of this wonder-woman. We kissed and I noticed that her hair had been pressed since the last time I had seen her and, even though I didn't agree with black women straightening their hair, she looked absolutely ravishing. We talked about how we each looked different and when I would be released, neither of us expressing the fear and the doubts about our relationship which we both felt. She told me about people and life on the outside, and how things were changing – her family, the job she was doing . . . But I didn't really hear, I just sat looking at her beauty. She noticed because she kept asking me why I was staring. By now I had an erection thinking about the times we had lain together and the way I had stroked her body, and I began to wish I could do it again. A small formica-topped table was between us and I couldn't even hold her, though I desperately wanted to, so we just held hands and looked into each others' eyes until a screw, walking around the tables, extinguished our daydreams with his 'Finish your visit.'

Even though it was said in a matter-of-fact and not unkindly tone of voice, nothing could disguise the brutality which would send my woman out into the world without me, and I back to my lonely cell with nothing to do except what I was told to do. Dolly looked at me and I at her, we didn't say anything but I could see she was on the verge of crying and the stab of pain I felt was indescribable. I should be there to protect my woman, look after her. How would she cope without her man? 'I love you,' she said.

Outside it was a dark December afternoon with the leaves falling and the wind blowing, everything looked brown and cold. How could I be a man not being able to look after and protect my woman, especially now that we both needed each other and longed for each others' arms.

'I love you, baby, but I think it is best that you don't come up to see me again. If when I come out we get together then that's cool, but at the moment I feel we should break up, and at least you will have some kind of life. What kind of life will you have with me?'

The tears appeared in her eyes as she registered what I was saying. She knew I loved her and didn't want her to stop seeing me, but she knew without me telling her that I didn't want her to see me in this capacity and I didn't want the shame or embarrassment of her having to come up and see me, of being subjugated to the role of a gangster's moll. I wanted to give her her freedom, to let her go, like a precious bird I was not able to look after. I wanted to release it into its own environment and for it not to be unhappy.

'I don't mind you having affairs but please don't bring any shame on me.' I turned and left with the tears in her eyes still lingering in my mind. I was in love.

When I got back to the cell I couldn't eat, and not because it was 'surprise pie'. The pie was so named because you would be surprised by what you could find in it; I personally found nails and even what looked to be part of an old sock in mine.

As my bed had been taken out and I wouldn't get it back until about seven, I lay down on my mat on the floor and thought about Dolly. We had first met about a year and a half ago in a club in Hackney when I had been firing. I was one of the boys, checked out in a smart suit with a shiny black Jag and with the confidence oozing out of me. I was governor, did what I liked, said what I liked and if you didn't like it, tough. I was a very arrogant young man. Money was never a problem and to pay to get into a club was unheard of for me and the boys, and in fact we actually liked people to ask us for money so we could go into our bad routine of pulling out our guns and letting one go in the ceiling. We thrived on the violence and people knew who we were. If you didn't, you soon did. We were your worst nightmare.

One weekday we all piled into my Jag and set off to a club in Hackney that we had heard about. All the boys in our firm were into some form of drug in those days. I had taken so many pills of different origin that I was out of my head, on what I didn't know. As long as it was a pill I'd get it down my neck. My friends were no different and that's how we arrived at the club, out of our heads. Being very arrogant young men with contempt for everyone else, we liked to go into clubs and stand right in the middle while everyone else stood around the edges, backs against the wall. You can imagine what the scene was: here were these guys from out of the area coming into a club where most people were too shy to stand out in the open and took to the cover of darkness by standing as far back against the walls as possible. We strode straight to the middle of the floor, well dressed and with plastic cups and bags full of drink, and began to dance without a care in the world or of what anybody thought. As the pulsating rhythms began we went into our extrovert dance routines to show that we were different and that we didn't care a hoot for convention. Soon we couldn't move because people were now all around us dancing and swaying along to the beat with us, infected by the excitement. We never chased women but let women come to us, we were real macho-men. Seeing men who to them were saying something different, women seemed to flock around me and my friends, some of whom were quite good-looking, and soon began chatting and dancing with us.

I saw two girls, one dark and one fair, standing next to me. I went up to the dark one, engulfed her in my arms and began dancing without a word. She didn't have a chance to say no, even if she had wanted to. All through the dance her friend, who by now had been asked to dance by my friend, was staring at me. When the record had finished, I turned to the fair-skinned girl and said, 'Why do you keep looking at me, do you fancy me or something?' To my surprise she said 'Yes'. Her name was Dolly and we danced away the night in each others' arms, both looking for comfort and someone to belong to, the warmth of our bodies wrapping us in a cocoon of togetherness. It was special and we both knew it. When at last it was time to go, she accepted my offer of a lift. After dropping my friends back at Ladbroke Grove I looked at her as I drove back to my place off the Harrow Road. 'I'm expecting a friend,' was the excuse I used to get her back to my flat. She seemed very beautiful, but more than that, her whole self showed an honesty and naivety that touched something within me. I promised myself never to hurt this girl or let her down. Even though I'd just met her, I knew that she was my woman, I felt it by the way she looked at me and smiled, God she was a beauty. The coming months were like a dream and every spare moment we had we spent together; soon I had met her brothers and sisters and overcome that barrier called mother.

As she lay on my chest in my flat one day she kissed me and said, 'T, I'm pregnant.'

Of course I pretended to be angry but was secretly pleased that a wonderful and beautiful lady who I happened to think a lot of could tell me she was pregnant; it made me feel so good. Of course I explained that I would stick by her. Anywhere we went I could be heard saying, 'Excuse me, please, my girl is pregnant.' The crunch came when her mother found out. She was sixteen and her mother wanted great things for her, as most mothers do for their children, and between them they decided to abort it. I just could not understand why, as a nineteen-year-old, and kept myself far away from the arrangements. I was obviously hurt, but what could I do? I had left home and was on my own. We got back together again and she seemed to need me more than before. I made her laugh but most of all I tried to make her forget, because I knew she still felt guilt. Even though I may have loved her, the macho image as a warmonger that I shared with my friends would not allow me to be in love. But I really cared for her.

There are some things I feel very strongly about and it's to do with the moral attitude of a lot of the young people in our community and for that matter a lot of the older ones too. Does anybody think that we as black people are exempt from criticism, or that because we can blame a lot of our problems on someone else we shouldn't take a close look at ourselves and stamp out some of the nastiness within the community? I understand how life can make one hard and not give a damn about anything or anyone else, and there *are* times when we should stand up for ourselves and be counted. But there's no need to be rude without provocation, there's no need to be abusive without provocation, there's no need to be foul-mouthed without provocation. It would appear that in the black community an aggressive streak with a foul mouth has taken over from calm reasoning. I don't like to hear children cursing on the street and abusing other people – there is no need for it, it makes us all look bad and it's slack, very slack. A lot of people who go on with that kind of slackness would not do so in front of their parents, they come out into the streets to do it. To all you people who go out on the streets, in the shops, on the trains and the buses and cuss anyone, even people who could be their mothers and sisters, let me say this: we don't need that in our community. We all understand that here we have to fight to live, to survive, but I don't want my neighbour robbing my house when I'm out, because if he does he's a thief, and we don't want people like that in our community. We don't want people robbing helpless women and girls, and abusing them, knowing full well that they don't go to the police. Well watch out, your time is up, we don't want you in our community.

We as men have a duty to look after and protect our women – how can any people be proud if their women are abused? We don't want petty people who are jealous of others – if you want something, go out and earn it. I'm tired of people who won't go out and do something for themselves, but just sit down and begrudge people who do. The only way they earn their money is by being sneaky and doing sneaky things, especially to their friends and people who trust them. And the joke is that these foul-mouthed abusers seem to hold some sway over the younger people of our community. Well let me tell you now, there's no pride attached to being aggressive, foul-mouthed and abusive for no reason. Just because you live in shit doesn't mean you have to be shit.

If you want to be somebody in life who can think and act

for yourself, then I suggest you leave behind any friend who's aggressive and abusive without provocation, and find your own way in life. We don't have to be killing one another, we don't have to steal from one another, we don't have to abuse one another – we can live like decent human beings. And if you can't, then we don't want you in the community and that goes for man, woman or child. I know we don't have much money, and I know the pressures we feel every day, but a lot of us experience it and fight it, and you too can be strong. Life seems empty and there seems to be nothing to do, you're restless, looking for something; but try your best not to get involved in things that you know deep down in your heart are wrong. Don't feel that just because your friends do something then you must do it – be a man and say no if you think it's wrong. The young are easily led and we the older generation have a duty to guide them, because they are only children growing up before their time. And if we see them in any danger or doing anything we know to be wrong and fail to save them, then we are *scum* of the most vile kind – it is wicked to stand back and watch them falling into a hole without doing our best to save them. When even adults have trouble surviving in such a crazy, mixed-up world, then think what it must be like for the young with so much temptation around.

I love reggae music because it tells like it is and those singers don't get enough credit for making our youth conscious and making them aware of who they are. Reggae singers, we love you! When everybody was fighting against you, you still stood firm and delivered the truth to us, and we thank you for it. But I believe the time has come when both singers and listeners should evaluate where we go from here. I've always known reggae to be a cultural music informing the people of what's happening and it's always been truthful no matter what. I was just thinking, that if some of the things I've said throughout this book you reggae singers believe to be true, then perhaps you'll join with me in reaching people's minds and souls with the truth, explaining to them that you can achieve whatever you wish, if you keep hope alive.

If we're not very careful we'll be sucked into a vacuum of hostility and aggression not only towards those we believe are our enemies but also towards ourselves. We're gradually losing our grip, our control. We are frightening the community, we are frightening our mothers and fathers, our brothers and sisters, our women and especially our children – we are frightening them with our own blood, their blood, and our dogmatic, unbending rigidity and inflexibility to reason politely, calmly and lovingly. Politeness costs nothing, and it's your duty, all of you out there know it's your duty, to behave with dignity, respect and honour – and if you don't, we don't want you in the community. If you don't we all know what's coming next – gang warfare and killings, we only have to look at America to see that. As with all under-privileged people, the lack of opportunities to channel our frustration can lead us to take it out on each other. But we can overcome that, we can channel that frustration positively in an endeavour to obtain our rights, and win respect for ourselves. We should be the protectors, not the destroyers of our community, taking responsibility, helping others in need, helping the children, helping women like our sisters. I detect an element of fear in the community at our male aggression, and I feel that we have to work together to show the rest of the community that their fears are unfounded. Don't be aggressive just for the sake of flexing your muscles, don't abuse people because you think you're bad. I know it's hard, but get into the swing of things.

Its like a jungle sometimes I wonder how I keep from going under.

It was now Christmas and the wing was a hive of activity. Even if the screws didn't personify the goodwill and spirit of

Christmas, they certainly seemed a bit more relaxed and that was the cue for some of us to sneak off to our friends' cells for hours. I remember hiding under a bed with three other guys covered by a blanket while a screw hunted for us. We were having something of a party because Beard, a friend who worked in the kitchen, and some white guys had made some hooch or rotgut concocted from potatoes, yeast and sugar; it was left to ferment and when drunk it turned your stomach over into a ball. I could just imagine my stomach rolling over in rebellion at such rubbish being poured into it, but hooch dulled your senses and made you forget. Someone produced a piece of hash and we all raised our plastic cups full of rotgut to toast the man as he rolled.

Christmas Day was really no different from any other day. We did get to see a film, but in essence it was business as usual. Just before Christmas I had been told that I would soon be allocated to a prison and soon after Christmas Day I was called down to the wing office to see the governor. He explained to me that I would be going to Albany, a maximum security prison on the Isle of Wight. I remember thinking, 'Where the hell is the Isle of Wight?' Anyway, at least I knew where I would be spending the next few years of my life. Of course we all discussed the possibilities of where we might be sent, but the Isle of Wight was generally passed over because we were lead to believe that it was for inmates who had already served a prison sentence.

We didn't travel by sweat-box but again by Transit van, the standard prison issue with barred windows. The fact that I had my own clothes on, creases and all, made me a bit happier. When you travel in a Transit you are handcuffed in pairs, not to the person of your choice but whoever you've been allocated to. It soon became apparent that none of us had ever made this journey before and the van was filled with the apprehension of going into the unknown. Unlike the claustrophobic sweat-box, it felt good riding in the Transit. Not only could you move your legs freely, but there was a good view out of the window and you could see all those lovely females walking by. Usually there were some rather lewd comments, but that day most people just looked.

I had learnt that we would travel to Portsmouth, where we would catch a ferry across to the Isle of Wight. When I heard that the Isle of Wight was not just a name but that it really was an island, I certainly began to worry. What was all this thing about it being a maximum-security prison? The Scrubs was like a fortress, but they said it was nothing compared to Albany. Where in hell were they taking me?

By now I had forgotten all my early ideas of escaping, but on that van ride down to Portsmouth the thought fleetingly came into my head again: I knew that once I was on the island escape would be virtually impossible. Even though I knew black people could be found everywhere, I had a sneaking feeling that not too many would be found running around the Isle of Wight except in Her Majesty's recreational grounds. The mere sight of my sneaking through the Isle of Wight after my escape would alert the islanders. Anyway, how would I ever get off the island? Steal a boat? How would I navigate? Where would I end up? With my luck I'd be washed up at the same spot I left from!

By the time we were nearing Portsmouth the fantasy of escape had given way to recognition of the reality. Albany was one of the three prisons on the Isle of Wight: the others were Camp Hill and the notorious Parkhurst, the mere mention of which made my blood run cold. Everyone knew about Parkhurst – I was glad at least that I wasn't going there. We knew that it was the end of the line once you reached Parkhurst. If they couldn't control you there, it was Broadmoor.

As we arrived at Portsmouth, the van pulled up at the dock and while a few screws went to organise things the rest of us sat in the Transit awaiting the ferry. Although there were many cars and people milling about, it seemed quite obvious that they knew who we were and where we were heading. People who parked their cars made sure they did so well away from us while those on foot made a big detour around our van, though they were eager to peer in from afar to see these real live villains.

All of a sudden I saw her staring at me. My first thought was to turn away but she looked straight at me and caught my eyes before I had a chance to do so. For several mesmerising moments we looked into each others' eyes. The sister was about the same age as me and looked African, but she was like a queen. Staring at me unashamedly as she spoke, she told me that she understood and knew what it was like. She called me her champion, her shining black knight, and told me that she loved me. With a ghost of a smile touching her lips, she raised her clenched fist ever so slowly across her chest and, as I did the same, a woman walked up to her who I assumed to be her mother. Then they turned and walked together back to the car. Even though I willed her to do so, she never turned around.

The van drove onto the ferry and we began looking around at the screws: surely we weren't going across in handcuffs. The man next to me started explaining to me that he couldn't swim and if anything happened, would I help him? I turned to the window and thought, my God, if anything did happen he would probably drown me with him. The cuffs alone weighed a ton and the door was sealed with several locks and bolts. 'We wouldn't even make it out of the door,' I told him, which seemed to make him a bit happier. 'That's true,' he said. He probably thought we'd all go with him.

The journey across was very rough and the rain began coming down, but I was a million miles away, my brain numb except for some soothing, relaxing waves of mellowed warm feelings. I was asleep.

My family and friends didn't know where I was, no one except the prison authorities; anyway, I didn't care. That's how our lives as black people had become, I thought. Most of us left home young or were thrown out after the inevitable clash with our parents: the old against the new, their old allegiance to this British society that they called the Mother Country, their Mother Country, where the streets were paved with gold; the front room parlours where you were not allowed to touch anything, and which most of the time were locked unless visitors came; watching your parents killing themselves for a pittance, growing old and becoming bitter, thinking the only way to train you was to beat you with the broom handle. We were rebelling against society's lack of respect for our parents and ourselves. Most black prisoners don't have any contact with their families and the best you can hope for is that a friend or girl occasionally visits you; but as most black men will tell you, the girls don't last too long and neither do the friends. Maybe it's because for black people every day is a struggle to survive and people don't have much time to worry about other people's problems. And in most cases parent-child relationships have been severed or left hanging by a thread.

We were now driving around the Isle of Wight through some winding country lanes. The rain had stopped but it was still grey as the van continued driving through the soaked roads leading us to doom. The prison stood on top of a hill, an awesome sight on the gloomy skyline. The nearer we drove, the more I knew I was now beginning my prison sentence, and for the first time since my conviction I felt subdued. I was completely drained and unsure of myself and the faces of some of the other prisoners showed they felt the same way. The van was quiet, as if we were being led to our execution. The prison was like something from the worst horror movies – I knew I would never escape from here. There was a fence about thirty foot high with masses of barbed wire on top, and as if that wasn't enough the fence itself was electrified and patrolled by guards with dogs. As we drove further in, we found that all gates were electronically operated. Next was a wall about the same height as the fence and maybe ten foot wide, with a huge rounded and overhanging top. This, too, was patrolled by guards with dogs. Still further inside the prison we faced a second electrified barbed-wire fence as big as the first. All the walls and fences had cameras on top and there were even what looked like infra-red rays placed strategically to trigger alarms at any movement. This wasn't an ordinary prison but a highly developed prisoner-of-war camp.

The whole prison was fitted out with the latest electronic equipment. It was like being taken to some secret planet that nobody knew about to work on highly sophisticated weapons – a fortress of security with doors and gates opening and then closing behind us at the touch of a button. The contrast with the century-old Scrubs was sharp and sinister. Albany was almost brand new, and clinically clean: the black and white tiles that covered the floor were spotless. We were herded into the reception area where we were fed, watered and given our prison clothes. The feeling of apprehension would not leave me, I was on edge and my eyes kept darting about as if looking for something. I was the only black person out of eight of us arriving that day. We had dropped another eight people off at Camp Hill, one of whom was a black guy, but I was the only one here, and the youngest.

After we had got our prison clothes and bedding and were waiting to be allocated to our wings, four inmates came in, and the way they looked and stared at me, I knew I wasn't going to like it here. They were all under thirty, with the confident cockiness that only comes with having already proved yourself within your environment. One of them, a blond-haired guy who looked like he spent most of his time in the gym, gave the impression that, whether outside or inside, he didn't know the meaning of fear, only death. It was obvious from the way this guy stared at me that black people didn't count for much in Albany, because he didn't seem to believe that as a black man I was capable of doing anything. While all this was going on the screws stood there, just watching. Although Blondie had three of his mates with him and I was on my own, I stared back without once taking my eyes off his. It may have been for no longer than thirty seconds, but it seemed like an hour that we stood eyeball to eyeball.

'Leave it out Tommy, you are always rowing, don't you want to get out?'

'The geezer was fucking screwing me,' said Blondie in answer to an old boy who had just come through the door.

By the looks of things this guy carried a lot of swing. He spoke with authority and seemed confident in himself. The arm across Blondie's shoulders signalled the end of the staring match and I turned before it could be resumed. I knew in here I would meet some bad guys and a lot of them badder than me. Blondie didn't just want to fight, he wanted to kill me, or at least injure me. The sweat was still on my forehead as the screws led us through to the wings.

I was allocated to B wing and as we got through the gate a voice said, 'Hercules, you blood clart you.' Standing in front of me was Bunny, and when we had greeted each other he began to tell me what was happening. I knew Bunny from outside, we both came from the same area in Ladbroke Grove. He had been convicted of armed robbery and was soon to be released. By now the screw who had brought me had left and another screw from the wing told me to follow him, 'Come on, sunshine!' I turned to the screw, 'My name is Hercules,' I said. He completely ignored me and walked on.

It was amazing, there were at least five black guys I knew in the prison, though we were not all on the same wing. That evening some of the boys came down to the wing gate and gave me shampoo, a toothbrush, soap, tobacco and a draw. Later on that evening, someone shouted out that there was a guy at the gate for me. 'Who is it?' I asked, and was told to go and see.

I couldn't believe it. Standing at the gate was Top Dog.

That was his nickname, his real name was Barry and we had been good friends outside – the first time I got into any trouble it was with him. Barry was over six foot and could fight, and I really mean nobody argued. If I say he thought very highly of himself that would be an understatement; and although nobody took liberties with him he had a heart of gold. He really was one of the boys. We had so much to talk about that we arranged to meet on the exercise yard the following day, and before he parted he left me a handful of goodies.

My introduction into Albany hadn't been bad at all, but there was always a feeling of tension about the place. The boys pointed out some real notorious villains – cases I had read about – but others, even though they didn't have the same notoriety, held just as much respect. Here, your name didn't mean anything because here there was nowhere to run; whether you were a millionaire or a bum, we were all equal, but I soon learned that some were more equal than others. This was cowboy country, where we, the inmates, made our own laws and dished out the punishments. The screws were there for one main purpose and that was to deal with trouble *after* the event. Otherwise they sat on the landing reading books or talking among themselves. You soon learn in prison that you don't talk to the screws, for if you're seen talking to one about anything other than a necessity you may be labelled anything from a grass to a spy.

Here, they didn't talk about things being wrong but 'out of order'! Liberty, turd, slag, nonce – there was a whole new prison language and the men who spoke it were something else again. A lot of the men were Cockneys, or if not Cockneys in the true sense, they came from London. Most had experienced the hard life and they themselves had now become hard. The clothes didn't help, the uniformity of the cloth only goading people on to rebel to show that they were individuals. These were men considered too dangerous to be let loose on society, bad men thrown into a pressure cooker and left to stew. The only time the screws acted was if two people shaped up to fight, and even then they wouldn't act until midway through the fight. Sometimes they would turn a blind eye altogether to what was happening. You could see their point: why bother getting injured when all they had to do was sit down and collect their pay packets? The bells that were placed around the wings were for the screws to press whenever there was any trouble, but the inmates took to ringing them, 'so the screws could earn their pay'. It was great fun to watch the screws tearing around the wings like chickens who had lost their heads. While there, I personally saw at least three screws have heart attacks – and all the inmates cheered as they were carried away on stretchers. Hard men, hard games!

The prison was made up of four wings with maybe a hundred men to each wing. Each wing had three landings with normal- sized cells; the main difference from Brixton or the Scrubs was that it was one man to a cell, as was the case in all long-term maximum-security prisons. That at least was a relief after sharing a cell with two others and their smelly piss-pots filled with do-do. After months of living in an atmosphere of sweaty, smelly bodies, to have your own cell was like having your own penthouse – even if your only pieces of furniture were a bed, table and chair, and of course the inevitable piss-pot. I also discovered that you were allowed to have certain luxuries in your cell as well as your radio (as long as it didn't receive VHF so you could pick up the police). You could have curtains, pictures on your walls, pieces of carpet and an eiderdown, as well as a portable battery-operated record player; and if you received special permission you were allowed a budgie and an acoustic guitar. These things may sound like luxuries, but they weren't much to men doing life, double-life, or thirty years.

Twenty years recommended was common, and many of the people inside would never be released. Prison was their life, the only life they would know, they would die here. My seven years was a pittance in comparison. The fact that sentences were so long meant that we all had to live with each other for a very long time.

To avoid trouble in a long-term prison means observing unwritten rules and following prison etiquette, because trouble here means serious trouble. There is none of that crap about punching a man in his mouth and then saying sorry, no abusing or threatening someone without following it through. If you had something to do, you did it, because such was the macho pressure of preserving your pride and saving face that if you didn't do what you had to you could find a knife in your back or boiling hot water from the urn poured over you while you lay in bed. There were items that people who had been there for a long time considered their own, even though they may have been communal, so you had to tread carefully. For example, even a tennis bat could lead to murder, and I mean real murder. Imagine a guy who has been in prison for eight years and every day at the same time in the evening he plays table tennis; he has been doing it for years, so he keeps bat and ball in his cell. You want to play, so you look for the bat and ball but of course can't find them. You then go down to the office and ask for another set, only to be told they've already provided bat and ball for this wing and regulations say they are not to let out any more for a month. So off you go to find the person who has them. You seek out the guy and ask for the bat and ball and are told, 'I'm going to use them soon.' 'Soon, when is soon?' Anyway, you may persuade him to let you borrow them, but the next thing you know you are halfway through a game when he comes along and says it's his turn to play because he always plays at this time. He looks you in the eye and you know he intends to play now, so what do you do? It's a very tricky situation, and many such incidents have nearly resulted in loss of life. When one party has got nothing to lose and may be in for murder, another corpse won't make much difference. After all, what can they do with a man already serving a double life sentence? In prison there's a very thin line between insanity and sanity.

The way the system combats the threat of complete anarchy from the prison inmates is by manipulating remission and parole. It works like this. Whatever sentence you are given you need only actually do two-thirds of it – so for me, doing seven years means I really do four years eight months, with the remaining third remitted providing I keep out of trouble. Parole, for which you are eligible after only a third of your sentence, is an even bigger carrot, although getting it depends on outside circumstances as well as behaviour inside. Together they comprise a powerful incentive to conform.

The workings of parole were always a complete mystery to me because if you were refused parole they did not have to give a reason why. Even if you were willing to change your attitude, you had no idea what was wanted.

Nearly everyone who worked for the prison service would provide a report on you when you came up for parole. The landing officer, the assistant governor, the welfare person who was stationed on the wing and was a civilian – all wrote reports; then there was the vicar; and last of all a parole interviewer who came into the prison from outside – someone you didn't know just doing some ordinary middle-class job. Where they were dug up from we were never told.

Albany's daily routine was the same as in other long-term institutions. Unlock about seven for breakfast, then locked up until about eight-thirty, when we were let out to work. Work consisted of a variety of jobs: there was the wire shop, where you made wire bows like in dickie-bows, for what I don't know; there was the paint shop, where you painted toy soldiers; the laundry and kitchen; the machine shop, where you used sewing machines; the carpentry shop; and then you had wing cleaners. We stopped work at twelve for dinner – when we collected our meals from the hotplate and ate them in our cells alone – and were unlocked again at one to go back to work. We finished work about half-four to five and were then banged up with our tea till just after six o'clock, when we were unlocked for association. This was the time most of us looked forward to, as we were allowed to roam around the wing, go into each other's cells, play cards or other such games, and so on. Downstairs they had a television room and table tennis; there was also an area for cooking, with a single electric cooker. We were able to purchase food from the canteen with wages. Between half-eight and nine we were locked up to start all over again. During the summer we were allowed on the exercise yard until eight o'clock.

I had been in Albany only two weeks and already could see the whole prison regime was riddled with racism and prejudice; not that it had been absent in Brixton or the Scrubs, but here it was blatant. It is very hard to describe racialism to someone who doesn't fully understand it or who has not experienced it, because racialism comes in many forms. Sometimes it's quite obvious, but more often it's more subtle and perhaps if you tell a person they are being racist they wouldn't understand. I myself do not care if someone claims to dislike me because of the colour of my skin, but what I do object to is when they start interfering with me without good reason and making my life a misery because of it. Whenever we black guys were hanging about during association we would get screws following us about and asking us, for no reason at all, what we were doing and where we were going. During association when you're allowed to roam about you might be coming downstairs when a screw would step right into your path and say, 'Where you going?' Or while getting ready for work, one would come into your cell and say things like,

'I'm giving you a direct order to get to work.' This usually preceded being nicked, even if there were lots of other people also getting ready for work. The worst screws were those with highly-polished boots and the peaks of their caps pulled over their eyes. A few black guys could not hold the pressure and they took to staying in their cells most of the time, visibly wilting as time passed on. The only defence against these bullies was to take matters into your *own* hands, because our countless appeals to the governor, either as individuals or as a delegation, fell on deaf ears, even with the statistics we had gathered up and presented. How was it that one screw could place six people on report in one week, all of them black and some not even on his wing? How was it that at times the block was full of people, all black? Why was it that when you reported being called such derogatory names as coon, wog, nigger or black bastard nothing was done?

Albany, like most long-term prisons, had a policy of excluding black inmates from work in the kitchen. Why this was or how it came about I don't know, but it remained a very strict institutional feature. The average prison earnings were about £1.70.

Mealtimes were very tense, often due to the fact that a large proportion of the black inmates were Moslems, yet the diet they were given often contained pork, much to their annoyance; they were told to eat it or go hungry. Eventually most of the other prisoners would be locked up, leaving those on Moslem diets still remonstrating about their meal. More and more screws would appear from nowhere with smiling, smirking faces, anticipating the principal officer telling them to remove these prisoners. Trying to stick up for your right to be Moslem and eat a Moslem diet, but at the same time knowing you were one of a few men trying alone to confront the system was dispiriting – the consequences could mean not only loss of remission but real physical harm when the swarm of blue uniforms moved in. There was nowhere to run, just a sea of blue uniforms.

After some time in Albany the tension that was every-where become very evident. Nearly every day there were fires. It was commonplace for someone's cell to be burned out and other parts of the building were not spared. Fights erupted continually as individuals settled old scores. The alarm bells rang constantly and you were forever looking over your shoulder, because even though you may not have had any trouble with anyone, your whole body and senses were on full-time alert and the pressure really confused and confounded your sense of equilibrium. Fire engines from outside seemed to be part of prison life, because no sooner had they gone than they were called back for some other emergency. This continual violence in an enclosed area, with gates and cells locked and the knowledge that if any-thing happened you'd have to rely on the screws, didn't appeal to me at all. The effect it had on the screws was to make them even more irritable and tense, and some were obviously frightened because they themselves never knew when some missile or object would be hurled in their direction when their backs were turned. Two men in our wing were stabbed, and another had hot boiling water poured over him – the way his skin peeled off just like some ripe tomato sent shivers through me as he screamed and writhed about on the floor until the men in white coats came and took him away. The men in white coats were medical screws with some first-aid knowledge.

It seemed that all the warnings I got from Top Dog and others about staying close and not mixing too much were good advice. The bloke in the next cell to me I learnt was very changeable and very unpredictable; as Top Dog said, 'I shouldn't have it with him.' So any time he tried to make conversation with me I just uttered the odd monosyllable and was on my way. One particular day he asked me if I wanted to read the newspaper he had, but I lied and told him

I had already read it. I didn't understand why I should lie because he seemed all right, but I remembered what Top Dog had told me. Anyway, he gave it to a guy called Paul in the cell opposite him. Several people saw him lend it to him, myself included. That same night he stabbed Paul, claiming he had stolen the newspaper. Paul was rushed to hospital to have several stitches put into a wound in his side. I was in a madhouse.

Chapter Four

I love sports and my first love is football. I pride myself on my football skills, so when I found that there was a series of matches about to be played at the weekend I thought, this is more like it. At last I felt a bit happier. These were to be international matches: Wales, Scotland, Ireland, England and the All Blacks. The whole prison was buzzing with excitement at the prospect of these matches.

Top Dog was captain of the All Blacks. As well as being an exceptional footballer who had once had a trial with Fulham, TD had pride in himself as a black man and no way could he bear our team to lose. The day before the match, we were both walking around on exercise together and TD explained to me the serious nature of what the match really meant. He said the only match that really mattered as far as the prison was concerned was England versus the All Blacks: 'It's more than a football match, they want to show their macho superiority over us and so you know we can't lose!' He also explained that it would be rough.

'The whole prison will be cheering them, Trevor, even the screws will love to see us lose and I don't know if some of our guys can handle it. They can play football, but when it gets rough and your back is against the wall, who knows?' TD had already proved himself by knocking out a few of the so-called 'chaps' and earned a lot of respect and, as his pal, it elevated me in the prison hierarchy. TD went on: 'I don't know about the rest, Trevor, but I know you and I have a lot of pride and dignity. I never want to be a bum, Trevor, and if we let these guys walk all over us tomorrow that's what we'll be. They're gonna be sending out their biggest bullies and henchmen onto the field, not footballers but fighters. They think we're afraid of them because they're villains. Well, if they are white villains, then we're black villains!'

And so the two of us planned our strategy in hushed secrecy as we went round and round and round the exercise yard.

TD explained that as a straight football match it would be no contest: we would murder them. But they would put plenty of physical pressure – blatant kicking and punching – on most of our team to put us off.

'They will be wary of me,' said TD, 'because they know I'll steam straight in, no mucking about. Once it's one against one I can't interfere for anyone and they know that, so they'll be testing you out son. Inside here, once two guys are fighting you let them fight it out, that's the way it is. If your friend gets done then you can do the other guy later. Unless it's more than one against one involved, you just watch, even if I'm fighting, because they'd love the chance to have a go at me firm handed so they could plunge me. But I know you'll perform well son.'

Our plan, or rather TD's plan, centred on their main hatchet man Terry, who was labelled a lump. He used the gym regularly but couldn't play football to save his life; he just stood in the midfield and kicked anything or anybody that moved, period – even his own men when they wouldn't pass the ball to him. TD said he would take care of Terry by being anywhere he was. I've already said I rated TD's fighting ability, but Terry was an animal and I was sure there would be some form of confrontation between the two. Even though I mouthed other ways of planning without TD sticking to Terry, we both knew TD's was the only way; he knew I really wanted it that way, but as a friend I had to make the appropriate noises. TD reasoned, 'You're a surprise package, Trevor, they don't know how good you are and by the time they do, it will be too late. But make no mistake, they'll try and do you.'

For the rest of our exercise period we walked around in silence, both lost in our own deep thoughts. Yes, I was afraid. I had fought men who had knives in their hands while I had nothing, been fired at by a man with a gun, yet here I was on the eve of a football match and my stomach was turning over. Though I value my body it was not for my physical self that I felt fear but for my pride. As a youngster, every time I saw black people competing I cheered them on. Even if I wasn't in a position to encourage them verbally, my heart always wanted them to win. It helped lift me and gave me a sense of pride and dignity, as if it were me who had been the victor, because the more black people achieved the more we as a race achieved, elevating ourselves in world-standing and standing not just for the bad things that this society is so quick to blame us for, but for good things too. What those black competitors achieved could stand as role models and could give others hope that they too would one day triumph. The worst thing I dreaded was letting TD down by allowing myself to be intimidated.

Because it seemed every gruesome murderer or robber ever to be written about in the daily papers was here inside this very prison, I knew trouble would find me even if I didn't want it to. That night I didn't get much sleep and my thoughts turned to my family – two brothers and sisters plus my father, and of course my mother. I loved my family dearly and had a very close and warm relationship with them all except for my mother, who I hadn't seen for many years.

They had all come up to see me when I had been on remand but the look of anguish and pain on their faces as they surveyed me from across the visiting table prompted me to vow to myself not to allow them to come up any more to see me like this. Besides, I was the one who had committed the crime, not them. Why should they be subjected to the role of prison visitor? I thought of their embarrassment at standing outside the prison gates waiting to come in as people passed by staring; and once inside, giving their names and addresses and being checked over to make sure they hadn't brought anything illegal for me; screws looking into my brother's face to see if they could recognise him from being inside, or assuming my sisters to be gangster's molls. I would spare my family the indignity of the prison regime and the terrible claustrophobic atmosphere of the visiting room. As we parted I explained that though I loved them I didn't want them to come up any more or write to me; but I assured them I had ways of contacting them and I would do so from time to time.

As on most weekends, the atmosphere became somewhat more easy-going and I awoke to my next door neighbour Jimmy's record player sending out the hypnotic sound of Bob Marley singing 'Slave Driver'. As the mellow sound touched me I felt good and relaxed and I knew during the game I would be all right. The matches were to start around ten. TD, who had been handing out the football kit to the players, finished about half-nine, then came into my cell where Norman and I were changing. We all dressed in silence, thinking of the job ahead. We had already gone through our plan with the rest of the team so there wasn't much point in going over it again. As TD began putting his socks on I saw him reach across the bed to his trousers, from which he produced a small knife about five inches long and shoved it down his sock. At first I thought I might be mistaken, but TD turned to me and asked me if I had a blade. Before I could answer him Norman miraculously produced his own blade and he too shoved it into one of his socks. 'No, I haven't.' 'I'll get you one before we go out,' TD said. TD looked long and hard at me and I knew what he was thinking. If he had talked to me he would probably have said something like, you've just arrived Trevor, and I know you can look after yourself, but in here there are some animals the like of which you've never experienced and they don't respect anything or anybody. If they get you, they'll kill you, DEAD. Just as we were leaving the wing TD passed me a knife and as the cold steel touched my palm my heart began to beat faster. I was still afraid.

The road that led me to prison could in many ways be considered the standard route by which black people get to penal institutions. Neither I nor my friends ever set out to be criminals or villains, nor wished to go to jail. But such is this society's evil hatred of those who are not of their pigmentation or their beliefs that we had no choice but to rebel against the system. We knew we didn't want what they offered, we knew they were hypocrites towards us black people; we were lost in darkness and we rebelled to find our identity, discover who we were. A lot of people may not understand fully when I talk about maintaining identity; for others the mere mention of black identity will conjure up visions of black uprisings, black power, killings of whites and other such foolishness. Any time black people begin to talk about their own culture, most white people begin to squirm and become uncomfortable, because they don't really wish to acknowledge that *we* have our own past and our own history quite separate from that of slavery and all that has been born out of slavery. Society has a deep-rooted fear of black people, and especially of the black male. Put boldly and taken out of context, this may seem quite absurd, but nevertheless it is true. The meaning of black identity is very difficult to describe to someone who's not black because even today there are many black people still trying to achieve their own sense of identity, and until they do they will always rebel against this society. Society shouldn't be afraid of us attaining this sense of identity because, contrary to popular belief, we don't wish to kill whitey, we just want to be proud and aware of our own cultural heritage and not become clones of the white man and his heritage.

School for black children in this country is a very traumatic experience – most end up never knowing whether they're coming or going. Hard to believe as it may seem, a lot of black children in their formative years at school believe they are actually white, and it sometimes comes as quite a shock to them to learn the truth. How can that be? Well, the whole of our education system is geared for white pupils, and doesn't take into account the thousands of black children who attend schools all over the country; children who were born here and will not just disappear after leaving school; children who will need jobs and accommodation in this society – in short, children who will help shape this society whether it be good or bad. Society will have to deal with young black children whether society likes to or not, because black people are here to stay. If they are to play a part as members of this society rather than as outcasts from it, one can see how important it is for these youngsters to have an awareness of themselves as people with pride and dignity, people with a knowledge of their true history and culture, as well as that of others. How can people know themselves if they know nothing of their past history and culture? Black people need to be proud of their past heroes and civilisations, and of their contribution to world advancement.

The British education system holds all other peoples of the world to be inferior, and they reserve their most contemptuous views for black people, whom they consider to be bottom of the pile. They dismiss and ridicule everyone's

culture and history as primitive and uncivilised. The fear
that society holds is that of the black man rising up against it
in retribution for the atrocities of slavery; hence in schools
they never teach us any of our history but just leave a gap
which implies that slavery is the only history we do have.
They state clearly that though things were bad they weren't
that bad, and go on to portray us as a fawning and childlike
people with rolling eyes so as to humiliate us into being
ashamed. They teach us that they did what they wanted to
us, raping the pride of our women and treating us no better
than animals, so that we as black people would feel so
ashamed of ourselves and our race that we'd want to forget
slavery as quickly as possible. That is why a lot of black
people don't want to know about their history and culture
because they think that's all there is to it; before that, the
white man's history claims, we were savages. All this brainwashing dished out by British schools to black people helps
keep us down, because people who have no pride in their
heritage have no pride in themselves. They have no heroes
and role models to follow, and what good is a race without its
great heroes and triumphs?

By hiding from us the wonderful, colourful characters of
our ancestors, the great kings and queens who ruled our
great empires and the warriors who protected them, they
have tried to deny us the rallying point which could make us
proud of our race. Still they fear that if they tell the real truth
about the atrocities their forefathers committed we will rise
up and rebel. So society hides our true history to demoralise
us.

Black bastard, wog, nigger, monkey, jungle bunny,
savage – just some of the names we were called by other
schoolchildren as well as by adults. Why should people be
calling us these names? They call us these names because
that is what they are taught by society, every aspect of
society. The mere fact that this country could produce
programmes such as 'Till Death Do Us Part' shows that this

country has no respect for us whatsoever. When people on the television call black people wogs, coons and jungle bunnies as part of a comedy show it is an insult to black people; and yet people turn around and wonder why black people don't want to be part of this society.

I grew up never knowing anything about my own black history, thinking the only history I had was that of slavery. And when the lesson came round to slavery I was so ashamed that I slid down in my seat, wishing the floor would swallow me up, especially when they showed what appeared to be these ugly, subservient black people lying on the ground with some white man's foot on their head. Many a time I went home and lay down crying into my pillow, ashamed of being born black, ashamed that my people were slaves, I hated black people for allowing themselves to be slaves. As if that wasn't enough embarrassment to be heaped on my shoulders, we then had a series of lessons on the Commonwealth and Africa. The whole of the black race seemed to be in turmoil, only able to help itself through the grace of white people; in effect, they got hand-outs. Then followed films of black people in the jungle, naked, living in what amounted to squalor, disease-ridden and hungry. In fact, as our teacher said, they were uncivilised. There followed another bout of embarrassment. There was never any explanation of how or why they were in their predicament, nor of how a culture that is different need not be inferior, nor of these people's past histories, nor what, if any, contribution they made to the world. To be honest I think in those early days I really longed to come from a race of people who were brave and proud. As I look back it seems those days were filled with embarrassment and loss of confidence.

About this time or soon after, I began to get myself into a lot of trouble, mainly because I wanted to prove to myself that I wasn't a mug, a black mug, I wasn't any slave. I started to have fights in school, usually caused by older boys calling me names such as coon, nigger or wog. I soon stamped that out with my fists and quickly earned a reputation as the best fighter in school. I was the boss, I was the governor, no more black bastard – I had respect. I became one of the boys in order to survive the hurtful taunts. I was the leader and if there was trouble, you could guarantee I was in the thick of it, and no one called me any black names.

As we warmed up on the pitch it seemed as if the whole prison had come out to witness this spectacle. I looked at the crowd without seeing anyone: there was just a sea of nameless faces and I wondered what I was doing here. The freshness of the morning air only added to my miserable frame of mind as I came up in goose pimples, and I remember thinking that after this prison experience I would never be the same. How could I, after all I had been through in the relatively short time I'd been in prison? Would it help me to be a better citizen? I reasoned that it never could, though it might well make me a very cold, hard individual. I decided there and then that prison was only for containment.

The referee blew his whistle and we kicked off in our opening game against Scotland, while on the other pitch England played Ireland. Our game was a scrappy affair, hard and littered with a lot of fouls, but the game was more or less fair.

Our next opponents were Ireland. My time in prison had shown me that the Irish and black prisoners had a good relationship in so much as they both believed that the British were prejudiced against them, and our game proved to be a good-natured match with both teams giving each other a lot of respect.

As expected, England and the All Blacks met in the final. The faceless crowd came alive. The game was only minutes old when the referee blew for a foul and was immediately attacked by an English player. As the two struggled on the floor it was left to the players to part them – since the referee himself was a prisoner he got no sympathy nor support from the screws as they stood and watched. The match turned dirty and vicious unlike any match I had played in before.

I remember the crowd being very influential in the match as they screamed and shouted on the players for greater commitment, and cheered loudly as players confronted each other and squared up. They hadn't come to see a football match, they had come for trouble. They had come to see violence, to see their fellow men hurt and injure one another. They were animals caged on an island and the football pitch was an arena where violence went on show. TD earned himself a lot of respect that day, courageous as a lion and tenacious as a terrier in shadowing Terry. As for myself and the rest of the team, we acquitted ourselves with a lot of respect and pride, and even though I had only been there a short time I sensed it was a turning point in the relationship between black and white. The way the black guys greeted us as we left the pitch and talked excitedly as we walked back to the wings told us we had done them proud. We hadn't been intimidated or frightened, nor had we respected the idea that we should fear white man because he was the villain who had firms and fired guns. We had come of age and we were now black villains, and the white guys knew that a milestone had been reached. Our relationship had changed; not that they were now frightened of us, but they gave us respect because we had earned that respect. Who won the match or what the score was didn't matter. What mattered was that a confrontation had taken place, a hard physical battle, and we, the black team, had gone into the arena representing not only ourselves and the black people on the wings, but all black people in prisons. We had come out with honour, we were a new breed of black men, a new generation of proven and recognised black villains. The white guys now knew that and afforded us the same courtesy one villain offers to another.

And perhaps in many ways it was inevitable that we should try to live up to the role of black villain.

The days, weeks, and months rolled on by and I decided to forget about time. After all, one day or one week was the same as the next. Time has no meaning in prison, not in hours, days, weeks or months, and if you ask a prisoner what month it is not many will be able to tell you. Who wants to know the date is 7th April 1976 when your release date is 1st June 1981? The days became monotonous, one sliding into the next, except for weekends when there was no work. I became bored and restless, moving from one cell to another until chatting also became tedious to the point where seeing the same faces day after day drove me to hide in my cell. I read books, listened to the radio, and read more books. Much to the horror of my near neighbours I purchased an acoustic guitar from a guy for two ounces of tobacco and for a time I was bored no longer, the thrill of learning to play keeping me occupied for hours and carrying me into a world of my own.

Prison is a lonely life. You arrive on your own without your real friends and family and the people you do meet in prison you mostly tolerate as opposed to welcome. It's lonely because you and you alone have to come to terms with your freedom being taken away, with being locked up and confined in jail. Other people don't wish to hear your problems, they've got problems of their own. A late letter or a cancelled visit is enough to give a prisoner a nervous breakdown wondering what happened. Are they all right, why didn't they come, why didn't they write? Your mind, already wracked by prison tension, becomes alive with ill fate. Only you can deal with it and you had better be strong. You feel so frustrated when you receive a letter or visit and something's happening out there which you could have prevented if you had been free. You feel so useless at not being able to help your family or friends.

I suppose it would have appeared strange if you could have seen the transformation I underwent during that period. I now took to the role of villain like a duck to water and my vocabulary quickly extended to words like wrong-un, grass, nonce, liberty, hold-up, and other such prison jargon. From then on I knew the rules on how to survive with dignity, but I also knew that to retain that dignity and pride might cost me my remission. Everyone wants to be accepted; I was no different. Because of the colour of my skin I was even more determined to stand up for myself as were other black guys: we knew the score, but were willing to pay the price for our pride and dignity. The price I paid was that I soon began to get in more and more trouble to retain my self-respect, just like school.

It seemed to me that we as black people were always having to prove ourselves. Society offered neither respect nor dignity to black people, and it seemed as if the only way to have it was to go out and get it. Every incident now became a 'liberty' or 'out of order' and I had to confront such events head-on. For example, one day I had just came up to my landing after collecting my dinner. Everyone was locked up on my landing except two guys, one white and one black. The black guy, Belly, was arguing with a screw while still holding his dinner, while the white guy who was opposite him looked on, presumably having already eaten his dinner. Belly and the screw were still arguing as they saw me coming along with my dinner. I was now involved. If I had passed by saying nothing I would have been held in low regard, firstly because, as one of the boys, prison etiquette demands you poke your nose in on any screw/con confrontation to make sure that the screw is not taking liberties; and secondly because Belly was a black guy.

'If you don't bang up now you're nicked,' the screw said to

Belly; but Belly had some grievance and would not bang up, and I knew that today I would end up in the block.

'Get in your cell, Towery,' the screw said to the white guy who was looking on, but he didn't move.

'Get in your cell, Hercules.'

I didn't move either. The screw then gave us all a direct order to get in our cells. When nobody moved he pushed the alarm bell and blue uniforms came from nowhere to escort us to the block. It was us and them, no colour bar. For the time being we were prisoners united against a common enemy.

Not long after that incident, TD was moved and a part of me went with him. He had been moved to Wandsworth to be re-allocated to another prison because Albany, no longer able to control him, wanted him out. The final straw for TD came after he had been followed about one day by this particular screw who hated prisoners who made the mistake of barring TD's path on some silly pretext, whereupon TD spat full in his face. Spitting in someone's face may seem a very nasty thing to do, but – consider what it is like to spend several years confined to prison – and that does not mean all the prison, just your daily trips over the same pieces of space until you know every mark and crack on the floors and walls of the areas you're allowed to be in, your cell, the television room, your path to work, the exercise yard. Then imagine a man in a blue uniform who hates you and makes your life a misery following every step you take, watching you, and on the slightest pretext pointing his finger at you, shouting at you, barring your way, belittling you, embarrassing you. With a uniform of legality, the system's on his side, he's right and you are wrong. Might is right and you have nowhere to go, nowhere to run, no one to turn to for protection from the enemy, the prison system that makes your life hell. If you do not confront it, it will slowly but surely eat away your pride, your dignity and your manhood and leave you an empty shell of nervous hate and fear. They want you to fear the system, run for the system, jump for the system, roll over for the system. The man in the blue uniform represents the system and they allow him to terrorise you. You hate the man with the blue uniform, you hate the system. Is it any wonder you spit in its face?

I was sorry to see TD leave. Although half-caste he had managed to cross the barrier between black and white in this hostile environment, and no matter what anybody said behind his back they respected him as a man because he stood up for what he believed in. A few months before TD left, an incident took place that nearly led me to killing a black inmate. Arcos was his name, and I had known him outside before we came to prison. On the outside a friend of mine was having an affair with a girl from Harlesden and sometimes when he went to see her I would go along. I became friendly with one of the girls downstairs; she said she didn't have a boyfriend and I could visit her when I liked. One day around Christmas time I was lying on her bed when Arcos knocked and came in – he seemed quite surprised to see me there was as we knew each other. We said hello, but a few minutes later he left, looking to me a bit annoyed. I asked the girl if he had any reason to be annoyed and she explained that they had been lovers, but were not now, so I forgot about it. It seems Arcos did not.

Everyone was on exercise except five or six of us black guys who stayed behind to chat about the outside. Arcos and I began to play cards for Mars bars and he began cheating, so I told him I didn't want to play, whereupon he leapt to his feet and threw a punch that, while not catching me full in the face, nevertheless hit me. I stared at him and he at me. We were supposed to be friends, and as I looked at him I knew why he had thrown that punch: it had nothing to do with the cards but with the meeting several years ago in his ex-girlfriend's room. If any white prisoners were about I suppose I would have had to damage him seriously that day, probably to the point of putting him in hospital, because some weeks previously a white prisoner had called him a black bastard and he hadn't done a thing, yet here he was slinging a punch at me. That same white prisoner would never have dared call me such a name, but always treated me with the utmost respect. The other black guys cooled the situation and then it was time to go to work.

In prison respect is everything and how the rest of your peer group (prisoners) see and relate to you is a very important and integral part of your life. For a man to punch you in your mouth and get away with it would be considered a liberty: 'do him', 'cut him', 'stab him', 'knock him out', would be the order of the day. But as we two were supposed to be friends things were slightly different. He said he was sorry and offered to let me punch him in the face and the rest of the black guys begged me to forget it, as they knew full well I would not let him get away with it. They knew as well as him that I didn't just want to punch him back, but that I really wanted to hurt him, and he knew I would do it – they all knew I would do it. He begged me in front of everyone, saying he was sorry and that we were friends, so I hadn't lost face and could quite easily have forgotten it. But the fact was that at the time I think he believed he could get away with it. Also there was this white guy who'd called him a black bastard and he'd neither said nor done anything about it: that was why I was going to do him. A knife was smuggled out of the kitchen for me and when it went missing everyone knew it was me who had it. I hid it on top of the water tank in the recess. I didn't know what I was going to do to him, but I was definitely going to do something. We were in our own world with our own laws – it was a jungle in which the strong survived, the fittest of the fittest. People came to me saying, 'He's wiped his mouth, Trevor, he doesn't want to know his rings flapping.' 'Forget it, T, he is your pal.' 'T, you can't do that.'

But I was going to. I was possessed by wrong-un, turd, liberty, nonce, rat; I was taken over by the institution. I was part of the prison, part of the walls, it was inside me, under my nails and in my heart. It possessed me until I didn't have a mind of my own. I was caught up in the aura and even if I wanted to I couldn't stop.

By now Arcos was a nervous wreck, what with looking over his shoulder all the time and standing with his back to the wall, eyes darting everywhere, looking for my presence so I couldn't creep up behind him. He had nowhere to run, nowhere to hide. Outside you can punch, stab, shoot or hit anyone and run away; inside you go nowhere. I didn't have to say anything to him because he knew I was going to get him, he knew me and what I was like and knew I would gain revenge. He wasn't made of the same calibre as me – he wanted parole, he wanted to be free, he wanted to go to clubs and rave, he wanted women and weed, whereas I wanted above all pride, dignity and respect. I also wanted to drive such fear of God into others that they would leave me alone and respect me. I was possessed by the evilness of a penal system that turned men into animals, trying to prove by the only way they could that they were men.

Today was the day, the day I would confront Arcos. I didn't plan it for any special day, but instinctively I knew it was time. I became immune to things around me as my body took on an unfeeling, uncaring numbness, a single-mindedness with one aim, one purpose and one objective: to hurt, inflict pain, gain respect.

I had no ties and no responsibilities, I was on my own. My family were OK and could do without me. My friends? Well, they were in the same predicament as myself, in jail. My girl? Though she had written to me, I had not replied. I was alone, alone to do as I pleased with my life. Whether I was right or wrong in what I was about to do didn't enter into it, all that mattered was that a liberty had been taken and must be avenged: God, reason, love of mankind – these had no place in my mind.

I decided to make my move in the afternoon after dinner. As I came down from my cell I saw him. I turned into the recess and reached my hand above the sloosh and felt for the blade which I had hidden there. As my fingers made contact with the cold steel it fell out of the back of the water tank, which I had assumed to have a cover, and fell into the bowl of the sloosh, going down, down, down, lost forever in that bottomless stinking hole. It happened so quickly that I didn't have any time to react and I just stood there staring into the sloosh bowl, feeling cheated, cheated by someone who was always against me, always robbing me of glory, always taking away satisfaction, never letting me enjoy my advantage. As I stood there staring into the sloosh my neighbour Jimmy appeared in front of me. He had obviously seen what had happened, but I had been oblivious to my surroundings and had not noticed him.

'Forget it, Trevor', he said, 'Jah works in mysterious ways. Maybe if it hadn't fallen you'd probably be doing life now. You got satisfaction, he said he was sorry and he begged you in front of everyone. You've nothing to prove and the people who are waiting for you to do him are only in it for their kicks. You are both black and I know you're a brother, T, with a conscious ideology and a clean heart and I know it grieves you that when he was called a black bastard he didn't do anything about it but you, his friend, he wants to punch. But you've terrorised him and made him beg, you have gained more than enough satisfaction.'

I didn't answer but turned and left the recess. Then I walked straight to Arcos and told him that if he ever talked to me again, I would kill him. He never did, and even until this day we still have not spoken one word.

Heavy as that confrontation may seem, violent confrontations within prison are regular occurrences. It was a man's world where only men lived, no women to make us soft and loving, no children to make us responsible and caring, just hard men, macho men, frustrated cocks who strutted around without hens.

We as black people can curse white man for the injustices he's caused us, for slavery – you name it and we can curse him for it until the cows come home. But in the final analysis we have to look at ourselves and if we are totally honest we leave a lot to be desired in the way in which we conduct our everyday lives. So what, we're under pressure. So what, we have a hard time. So what! Does that mean we have to forego our principles and morals because of that and act out the role, the label given to us? I say no! The first thing we have to do is to stop feeling sorry for ourselves and stand up and be counted. Each and every individual must take on the responsibility of being the men and women that we are without always hiding behind sterile excuses that we are downtrodden, discriminated against and racially oppressed, even though we are. Get up and shake off your chains of apathy.

At the moment a lot of our warrior men and our sisters are lying down and dying, wasting our lives away, doing nothing, saying nothing, just wasting away our lives. Be honest with yourself, what are you doing with your life at this moment? I know a lot of people out there will try to avoid this question with excuses about this and that and that and this, but you are lying to yourself, you are cheating. You are cheating your children, depriving them of the role models they need, depriving them of father-figures and mother-figures to look up to and respect. Be honest, what are you doing with your life? Go on, I dare you, if you call yourself a man or woman take a good look in the mirror and tell me what you are doing with your life. If you are fucking up, there's still hope, believe me; if you are fucked up, there's still a chance, because things don't have to be the way they are, you can change things for yourself, you can do things for yourself. Don't lie down, don't accept it because 'that's the way it is', because you can do whatever you want to if you put your mind to it.

I know a lot of people may feel away about what I'm saying and God knows I've fucked up myself, but in our search for truth we have to be honest with ourselves and with each other in an endeavour to find that truth.

Our day-to-day existence, survival, is no longer the most important thing; we have to move on and find some substance to our lives. It's no longer good enough just to exist, we must now begin to flower, to bloom, and to realise our true potential politically, socially, and economically, because we are drifting apart from each other, leaving only a void of hate, unconstructive aggression, self loathing and bitterness towards each other in our frustration at the lack of self-motivation and direction in our lives.

It seems we give up far too easily. We start something and then never get round to finishing it, so we just drift from one thing to another without any real stability; in other words, we are always trying a 'ting' and if something doesn't go right with it we just leave it and go on to something else. I know there's a lot of obstacles in our way, but if you start to do something and that's what you want to do then don't let those obstacles stand in your way. You've got a mind and intelligence, there's always a way round that obstacle if you really want to get to the other side; you and only you will know how much you want to get round that obstacle, but if it's really worth it you'll succeed.

The same applies to any shit or badness in your life: if you really want to overcome it, you will. It is wrong, a sin, just to lay down and accept things. If something's not right, then don't accept it, persevere until you get what you want because we all have a duty to ourselves and our children at least to try our best and not be selfish and take the easy way out, not to become sheep and just lie down and die.

We as a black community here in Britain, what do we really want? Do we want freedom? Do we really want to find our identity? Do we want to go back to Africa, the roots, the motherland, or do we want to stay? Do we just want equality, being allowed to live our lives as we choose like any other human being on this planet? It is individuals who make up the black community, and at the end of the day it is each and every individual who has to make up his or her own mind about what he or she really wants. It's no use being up in arms, shouting your anger and frustrations, being bitter with a hate that consumes your body, your mind, your soul, that leaves you an empty shell that wants to lay down and die. Only when we know what we really want as individuals can we pull together as a unit, not only to let our voices be heard but to achieve our goals as a people, to go forward in life and be in control of our own destiny. Once we know the path our lives should take, then and only then can we start to find a common purpose, a common goal and achieve self-determination as black African people, as a race.

The reason I put forward this argument is because of the apathy that exists in the black community, a don't-care, don't-give-a-damn attitude, with everybody only thinking of themselves. But there are generations to come after us, our children, our children's children – what are we going to leave for them? Is it to be the same suffering we endured, is it to be the same pain? Or do we wish to leave them with some hope for the future, something that we have built and that they can continue to build upon? Our children must be free to find their true identity away from that of slavery, free to take their true place on the world's stage and go forward to a better way of life and a better existence, free to control their own destiny as they feel fit, and not because they have no other choice or because 'that's the way life is'.

The secret is that anyone can be what they want to be or

achieve what they want; but that shouldn't necessarily mean financially – it should mean what you want from life, your own peace of mind, what makes you happy as a person, without that black element always rearing its head. As a people we are not really happy, we are not contented with our lives, we have no peace or tranquillity. For the most part we don't really live normal lives. Our relationships with each other are very precarious and friendship seems to be a whim – people change friends as they change shirts. The bonds between us have become very flimsy and usually depend on what one person can get from another. That is a very fragile state of affairs – relationships need to be based on trust, honesty, truth, friendship, loyalty, and yes, love! These are the things that stabilise people giving them character. We're always talking about this person was my friend but turned to stab me in the back. If we got a penny for every time we heard that story, we'd all be rich.

Stand up and take a look at your life, Mr and Mrs Black Individual, can you really face up to the truth, can you really be honest with yourself, can you? And if you are living a lie, cheating, can you be man or woman enough to change that, if not for yourself then for your children? There's no shame in having to admit to one's faults, we're only human. Everyone in the world fucks up. The world is fucked up, but we have to be men and women enough to admit to each other that we've fucked up, then we'll be able to set things to rights. Other people are lucky, they've got their leaders to pull them together in times of crisis; but we haven't really got any leaders to rally us around and give us strength. We've only got ourselves, so we really need to be close to one another, learning to trust and trusting, being honest and receiving honesty, expecting to be loyal and giving loyalty, respecting and giving respect, loving and being loved.

Losing one's way in life is easy, and seems to be becoming easier and easier. There are many of us in jail, reflecting on our lives and where we go from there. Then there are those who are unemployed, searching not only for the answer to their financial problems but also for their roles in life. Is this really what I want from life? I firmly believe that is the question we should really be addressing ourselves to. There are not that many role models to set our sights on – unless you want to be a boxer or an athlete or a singer – because there are hardly any professional people from the black community. And many black professionals who have made it have not done so on their own terms; they have had to lose something, their black identity, because they had to be acceptable to white society whether they chose to or not. I'm not on their case because in every field there has to be pioneers, people to lead us forward. But the difficulty is that to a lot of black youngsters they are not seen as role models, because it's as if they've disengaged themselves from us, forgotten who they are and where they came from, as if they are ashamed and trying to forget. This can be clearly seen in the fact that most black people who make it end up marrying white partners, as if we're not good enough for them any more – and to most black people that's an insult. We too may aim to become a lawyer or an accountant, but not to the extent of ignoring who we are. It may take longer but the secret is you can achieve whatever you want to if you want it bad enough.

That is why in the black community the role models we do choose are those who *have* retained their identity and they are mostly singers and sports personalities, not the ones that white society holds up for us, but our own heroes. We love George Jackson, Mohammed Ali, Malcolm X, Marcus Garvey and Angela Davies. These people have gone a long way towards erecting black pride, regardless of the consequences to themselves. There are white people we respect as human beings, like Mark Knopfler of Dire Straits who also refused to go to South Africa, and even refused to take any royalties from sales in South Africa. When I saw him on television my heart really went out to him to be a good human being. But at this point in time our heroes are black, but in years to come I would hope we will look up to people because they are decent human beings, not because of the colour of their skins.

Some people may not necessarily aspire to those professional heights in the attempt to find their way in life. Some may wish to find other pastures, such as the West Indies, Africa, or some other part of the world, even though they may have been born here. As we know, it's not that easy to get up and go, but the biggest stumbling block is mentally adjusting ourselves and overcoming our fear and prejudices. There *are* other options apart from living here, where so many people are unhappy and dissatisfied. You can go to where your parents came from and broaden your horizons. What have you got here? Most black people don't have lots of money – in fact quite the opposite is true, the majority of black people here are poor. So unless you have property or a business or plans of that kind, why stay? A lot of people are under the misapprehension that if they go anywhere else they'll be losing out, but if you've got nothing I fail to see what you'd be losing! Social life, nightclubs, parties? You mean those gatherings where at any minute the police can kick in the door and raid the place and take people away? Yeah, I suppose you would miss the excitement, wouldn't you?

In many of Britain's prisons a good majority of those inside are black, and most are guaranteed to return. When they eventually do leave prison, they will be considered unemployable. They won't have anything to show from being in prison, only the scars and a hatred of a system and society that is white-orientated and not geared for them. They will find themselves in limbo, just going through the motions.

Perhaps it's a time for a change of scenery. Cold weather and dry skin await you in winter here. You have nothing but radio and television programmes that have no real meaning or relevance to you, and certainly don't reflect your opinions. You are restricted to neighbourhoods and a social life by man-made boundaries, by stares of hardness and coldness and enquiring glances which say, 'What are you doing here?' Maybe I should say I'm British, but am I really?

The fear factor about leaving Britain is of going into the unknown. But black people are of African descent, and *Africa belongs to you.* One can understand the fear and apprehension because we are fed on a diet of black inferiority – educationally, politically and economically. But Africa is calling a lot of black people born here, so try and overcome that instilled fear of savagery and cooking pots and bones through noses. Enquire, seek proof, check out. Take a positive attitude and leave behind the negative attitude of a society which you may feel is not your own, because only with honesty and self-knowledge can you adapt to a new society. Just because you feel prejudice and maybe intolerance about a continent that was once raped, that doesn't mean it was the continent's fault, as any woman will tell you.

I hope that you will never be ashamed of what you see on the television – whether it be South Africa or Ethiopia, you shouldn't be afraid to confront it and see who you really are. If you are a human being, you'll find a way to help. If you can, you will. Don't complain of all those black stars with millions who have never given anything, only taken – it's for them to know themselves. Don't be prejudiced out of ignorance – find out about Africa, slavery, colonialism, and how and why it came about. Then the prejudices and inferiority complex that the media and others would like us to have won't be forthcoming. Most of all, we should never lie to ourselves or cheat. The secret is that we can be or do whatever we want.

Chapter Five

As time wore on in Albany, I found myself getting into more and more trouble, and to be quite honest sometimes I welcomed the block to get away from the tension of the hate-filled wing with its overpowering sense of hopelessness. Whether prisoners admit it to themselves or not, most of them become paranoid at times. After all paranoia seems to be an ever-increasing trait in our society, and within the confines of the prison institution, with all its rules and regulations and its action and interaction between people brought together for no other purpose than that they are considered bad by society, for inmates to be free from paranoia would somehow be totally abnormal. Prisons, and especially long-term prisons, have their own special tensions caused by the psychological interplay between prisoners and prisoners, screws and prisoners, screw and screws and even the governor and other workers at the prison. We all become entwined in the same web. One could almost consider it a game but for the seriousness of it, and the overpowering mental pressure of keeping to rules which are not only complex and subtle but, because they are nowhere defined, can only be learnt by bitter and sometimes dangerous experiences.

The claustrophobic intensity of every day being the same, of having nowhere to go, of seeing the same faces doing the same things, of having the same meals time after time – after a while it takes its toll. People begin to come under pressure and that thin line between sanity and insanity is stretched to the limit. The situation becomes rather delicate and your judgment is tested because you have to know when to talk to people and when not to. One word out of place to someone under pressure can lead to trouble, but how do you know when someone is not wanting anyone to talk to him? Usually when he tells you to fuck off. But not everyone makes it as simple as that.

Some people come under such extreme pressure that constant paranoia sets in and these people become extremely dangerous, believing that others are always screwing them (watching them), or always suspecting that someone has been in their cell and taken something. Once such an inmate takes a dislike to you, it's bad news. You may see them watching you from the top of the landing, and you in turn begin to get edgy, thinking they may come up behind you or come in your cell with boiling hot water to throw over you. Soon you too begin to get paranoid and, seeing your suspected assailant in a tête-à-tête conversation with someone, you believe they are planning something against you. Any misunderstood form of action by either party can then signal war.

To argue with anyone in prison is to have sleepless nights and paranoid days, because some people never forget, and also because people can enhance their reputation and their standing in the prison hierarchy by doing someone. In a macho environment, where male dominance and strength count, there is much incentive to be violent. The only reason why the violence is kept down is that even if trouble, when it comes, involves only two people, those two people may be part of different firms or have friends who will stick by them. That's why the people you choose as your friends in prison are all-important. The rest of the firm usually cool and reassure the person on the other firm that nobody wants any trouble but that if trouble starts then they will retaliate. Once everybody has proved they are not frightened by the other side, honour has been upheld and people can get back to some semblance of normality. The whole prison can breathe a sigh of relief, even the screws and workers and the governor, because when all this is going on the prison authorities are in a panic. Everyone wants to prove themselves and during these periods officers get much abuse and if they talk out of turn to any prisoner they are likely to get a right-hander. So the screws themselves get caught up in it, and they become apprehensive because they know they'll be sent in to try and control the situation if it gets out of hand. Men doing double-life are not easy to control, and at times like this a screw is just as likely to be done as anyone else. Other screws are drafted in and the place is on tenterhooks. Prisoners set off alarm bells and screws run around in a fearful state. The other prison workers make themselves scarce and even the governor keeps out of the way. For him to walk around the wing is to risk being spat at or having things thrown at him.

Even at normal times you're searched in prison when you've finished work, one by one, and your cell is checked every day, in addition to the spot checks which can take place at any time. But during periods of high tension the whole process is intensified. Everyone's cell is searched ('turned over') while its occupant waits outside, under guard. Personal objects are gone through with a total lack of respect. If you manage to survive without becoming a nervous paranoid wreck you've done quite well. For at least a month afterwards any sound behind you is cause for concern, and what paranoia you had before becomes so intense it makes you physically sick. Once again you begin to wonder, what the hell am I doing here?

The present prison regime must be changed to allow people greater freedom, because to be cooped up for so long in such limited space can only do harm and society will suffer for it, because in the end most of these people must be released.

Despite the pain and torment of imprisonment it was often the news from outside that stirred in me the greater anger. Repeatedly the television news showed us pictures of South Africa, people being shot, beaten, abused just as if they were animals with no feelings. In fact, had these people – these black people, my people – been animals, the world would have already stopped this evil regime. Often I would leave the telly room and walk out so angry that my whole body was shaking. Seeing the hate in my eyes, the screws move out of my path and stare as I kick a plastic bucket up in the air. They probably think I'm cracking up. I go into my cell and shut the door as hard as I can and the sound echoes. I lie down on my bed and put my face in my pillow and the tears roll down my cheeks as I cry for my brothers and sisters in South Africa, who reflect my image just like a looking glass, they are so much a part of me. How did I come to be here in this cold barren country where they do not respect me, nor my family, nor any other black person. I began to hate my parents and blame them for all my troubles. Had I not been born here I would not be in my present predicament in an alien environment where I feel all alone with these white beings from God knows where all around me. I imagine how the black slaves felt when they first set foot on American soil. They must have thought they were in hell, and believe me they weren't far wrong.

I realised then that not until South Africa is free and the rest of Africa is able to determine its own destiny without interference can we as black people be a real voice and power in world affairs. But Africa must rid itself of its colonial mentality, the guilty feelings of shame at being a raped continent. Africans should look across the water and see that their sons and daughters who were stolen are lost without their language or culture and are in the wilderness amongst a strange people in a cold land. Every race throughout history at some time has been conquered, there is no shame or disgrace in that. There should be no need now to be embarrassed because of slavery, even to the point where we somehow persecute ourselves subconsciously as if it was somehow our fault, or the fault of the black race.

Slavery was a fact, it happened. So what! We know all about what took place. Yea! Yea! Yea! I know all about those things! As long as you're conscious and aware of your own history, you won't let other people brainwash you into having an inferiority complex about your race, or most importantly, the colour of your skin. It seems strange the relationship that exists between black people born in Africa, and those of us born in Europe. Both groups tend to keep themselves socially separate and are quite content to co-exist side by side without really interacting. Each group's attitudes towards the other over the years have been filled with mistrust, suspicion, and at times outright hostility and aggression – the chains of colonialism and the effects of the divide-and-rule policy still linger. With the advent of slavery and colonialism, the imperialists encouraged one tribe to believe that they were better than the next and deliberately created borders in Africa that would result in tribal warfare. This was the basic policy of the Europeans: divide the people and divide the land. Divide and rule.

The legacy of this still exists today. Even though a lot of people have managed to shake it off, this division, this wall between Africans and captured Africans, has to be broken down before we as an African race can go forward. Captured Africans no longer revere Europeans – we know them for what they are, we know how they work, how they think, their strengths and their weaknesses, their goals and ambitions. Living amongst them, many of us have managed to de-brainwash ourselves of their colonial bullshit. Africans, however, who have not been as close to them as we have, cannot see their subtle caricatures, cannot penetrate their fork-tongued double meanings, their smiles and false friendships. They haven't learnt first-hand as we have, and they still suffer greatly from the attitudes of colonialism.

Africa and Africans try to dissociate themselves from slavery as if it had nothing to do with them, because they are afraid of slavery, it's a skeleton in the closet and it won't go away. They'll have to confront it sooner or later because we captured Africans are realising more and more who we are and where we came from – we're looking at Africans and then running to look in the mirror and we see that we are the same. You speak bla, bla, bla, we too want to speak, bla, bla, bla, you talk of your motherland, your country, we too soon will want to call it our own, because Africa is every captured African descendant's home.

It's a very difficult issue to deal with because the colonial mentality is so embedded in Africa that at times it may be hard for African descendants to understand it. Somehow, somewhere along the line, Africans seem to have come to believe that they are superior to African descendants, whom they refer to as slaves and West Indians, as if these labels somehow alleviate the guilt and shame they feel because Africa was raped and its sons and daughters were stolen and the continent was plundered and turned upside down into the turmoil it still suffers today. Many African countries look towards the West, or the Commonwealth, for help, and see America and Europe as a way out of Africa, which has been bled dry first by Europeans, then by corrupt African officials. Coming to Europe or America to find work and money, they seem to find it hard to understand how it is that we African descendants are not rolling in money. They can't comprehend what slavery was really like, nor the battles we fought not only to free ourselves physically, but also to break the chains of mental bondage. African people don't really realise the full horrors of slavery.

The mentality of Africans, I'm afraid to say, is still to some extent conditioned by colonialism. South Africa is a prime example. How is it that such a few people can invade your country, kill you, kill your children, steal all your wealth, and banish you to the edge of your country? Surely even the most placid person would turn and take up arms and be truly justified? But what do we find? We find both the army and the police force, the tools of oppression are filled with Africans. Not until they rid themselves of the colonial mentality can they step forward. Africans tried so hard to get away from the white man's view of the African savage, that they ended up copying and behaving like the European, even changing their names to European ones. Worst of all, they tried to pretend they had nothing to do with African descendants.

But slave mentality is also prevalent amongst African descendants, because it is hard not to be affected by something when its so frequently reinforced. It would appear that every time Africa is shown on the television it is shown in a bad light, with Africans unable to help themselves, fighting, starving. Our children read history and geography books in school which make Africa out to be something to be ashamed of – some African descendants actually believe the lie that their forefathers sold *themselves* into slavery; and some Africans are happy to agree to this lie because it enables them to feel superior.

But now both Africans and African descendants need to get together and talk, try to understand each other, their ways and customs. Though in Europe we live in close proximity to each other, we still go our own ways socially.

We both need to be close to each other, so African descendants can learn about Africa and its culture, while Africans can learn more about the ways of the Europeans and their lost brothers and sisters.

Africans and African descendants should have some form of rapport. We have a lot to offer Africa and Africa has a lot to offer us, so we should at least have some form of exchange programme, whereby people could go over to offer services or skills, in Ethiopia for instance. There's untold potential within the black community here, just waiting to be developed given the right circumstances and environment. In Sierra Leone, West Africa, I got into a heated debate when, after being told that most African descendants were thieves, I asked what would happen if all Africans went to live in Europe and America, and all African descendants came to Africa. I believe that the African descendants, with the knowledge they have of the world, would make Africa a success and find their true selves. I also believe that Africans in Europe would have a rude awakening to modern racism – that placid colonial mentality would soon be substituted by an aggressive instinct for survival.

Thinking about this, I ask myself: why did my parents leave their lands to come here? If they came for a better existence for their children, I challenge them on that issue because now many of their sons and daughters are behind bars, rebelling at being here. Most of their sons and daughters don't know their own countries and are now apprehensive of going to a place they've only heard about, a place their parents chose to run away from and seem never to want to return to. That is why we don't just rebel against this society, but also against our own parents who have been so brainwashed that they tell us this society is all right, and that we should behave ourselves and keep out of trouble. They ignore our grievances against this society. We rebel against our parents who tell us not to get mixed up in any black power business and not to read those black books that tell us about our history. We're angry at our parents who never sat down and told us of our true history, not that rubbish they taught at school. We rebel against our parents who every day curse black people for being as bad as their black skins. We curse them for giving us an inferiority complex by telling us how good the white man is, how clever and how smart, while dismissing the black race in the same derogatory terms they had learnt from the same white man. Yes, we rebel against that, we will always rebel against that.

We rebel against our parents' fawning subservience in the face of the white oppressor, that same white oppressor they cursed and cried about behind closed doors, yet told us wasn't so bad. Well, we rebel against all of that, we will always rebel because we know better. We know the truth. We rebel against the media which prints derogatory things about us, so the rest of society is brainwashed into fearing and hating us, while we in turn are not able to respond because we have no political or economic or media power. We rebel against this society which depicts us as savages, niggers, jungle bunnies, wogs and coons, and adds further insult to injury by allowing their comedians to come on telly and laugh at us before the world while we cringe with embarrassment and shame. We rebel against this society which allows its police to harass, beat and kill us in the name of law and order. We rebel against this society and its racist laws and policies, its hypocrisy in allowing and helping the South African government to inflict murder and other atrocities against our black brothers and sisters in their own land. Had the situation been reversed and it was black people oppressing the whites in their own land, white societies all over the world would immediately send in troops and drop bombs not only on South Africa but all over Africa.

We as black people know that you take us for fools and clowns, but the tables are turning, slave-master, and that is your greatest fear. As we freed ourselves in Zimbabwe, so we will do the same in South Africa. We rebel against society for destroying and hiding our proud history from us, stealing our historical pieces, arts and treasures and putting them into your museums as if they were your own. One day they will be returned to us, the rightful owners, so we can be proud of our forefathers, of our African heritage.

With these rebellious feelings constantly stirred by my growing awareness it was inevitable that I became a regular visitor to the block, and in those days in Albany it seemed I spent more time there than in my cell. I refused work on the pretext that the workshops they were sending me to were the worst in the prison. My regular confrontations with the screws were now getting out of hand, and at times I could be seen staring eyeball to eyeball with screws, insulting them with some vile abuse while my remission rapidly decreased.

Prisoners usually mix freely with other prisoners – except of course for the nonces (child molestors or rapists), grasses or other wrong-uns. The Irish, although mainly political prisoners, also mix freely, though they do stick together as well. I found that the Irish, contrary to popular belief, were intellectually and politically very astute. We shared many fascinating conversations about anything from politics to music and generally got along fine.

Myself and Jimmy were working in the wire-shop once, and getting continual reminders from the shop officer to keep working. Finally we told him that as we were on piece-work we could go as fast or as slow as we wished. With a smile on his face he said, 'I'm giving you a direct order to work.' We pointed out that there were people sitting down doing nothing and demanded to know why he was always telling us to work and not them. 'I'm giving you a direct order!' It wasn't planned and I don't know who made the first move, but Jimmy and I rose, simultaneously it seemed, and began to wreck the shop, smashing everything we could. Of course the alarm bell went, but by the time the heavy mob arrived we had caused enough damage to satisfy ourselves. Then we were escorted to the block where we would wait to see the governor the next morning. While on punishment for that offence we got talking to some Irish lads who were Provisional IRA. They had had a peaceful sit-down on one of the wings over some grievance and were now down the block; some had some very serious injuries, including one next to me with a broken arm. As I've said before, everyone in prison is being punished, and that is sufficient reason for some kind of bond. The Irish boys claim to be political prisoners, though whether others see them as that I suppose is down to the individual. I don't make any judgment on that: when someone gives up their life not for money or gain but simply because of political belief then they must believe that what they do is right and I am not their judge and juror.

The way that the Irish were treated by the screws disgusted me and Jimmy. While in my cell one afternoon I heard what appeared to be scuffling further on down the passage, and as usual people began to bang their doors. I didn't know who it was until next morning on exercise, when Jimmy told me he had seen a screw spitting in the food. Jimmy asked him what he was doing and was grabbed and locked in his cell. As the news spread it was decided we should go on hunger strike, because who wants to eat food that's had spit and God knows what else mixed in it? The hunger strike lasted five days, until the governor conceded that a prisoner from the kitchen should serve our meals.

The one thing I never want to do again is go on hunger strike. I don't mind most forms of protest, but I made it clear to the others that for me hunger strikes were definitely out. My body had never felt so weak in my life and I thought I would actually die, here in Her Majesty's prison. The thought made me realise that if I was going to die I would sooner die fighting than starving. Every mealtime the screws would come around asking if we were going to eat, and each time they did they were met with a torrent of abuse. It was the strangest sensation of my life, and during the strike I searched for my soul and bared myself open. In that dark, damp cell I felt like a condemned man. I didn't know what was happening, it was like I was immersed in something that I couldn't get out of, as if I were drugged and had neither the energy nor the will to get back to normality. When I hear other prisoners say, 'I've been there,' I fully understand them because, believe me, I've been there.

It may seem strange but my main concern was that I didn't show any sign of weakness to the screws, who believed Jimmy and me to be the weak links. They kept coming to our doors to try and 'talk some sense to us'. They came out with things like, 'Don't die with those Irish scum.' I don't know about Jimmy but sometimes when they came to my cell I'd drop my trousers and start masturbating, saying things like, 'Its good here, innit?' or standing in a corner singing reggae songs at the top of my voice. The Irish lads knew what the screws were doing, and though they didn't mention it I knew we earned their utmost respect. Even the screws who thought we wouldn't last realised they were dealing with a different generation of black men. These young black men who were coming into prison were hard, but added to that they were proud – and that's what the screws hated most.

I refused to come up from the block when my punishment was over. I told the governor that until I was allocated to a decent workshop, I would not work. By now they knew I meant business. They let me stay for two weeks and then the governor told me that if I went into the sewing shop for a week I'd be moved to one of the better shops. I agreed. When the week was up I still wasn't moved so I came to work and refused to actually do any. I just sat there for two days. Then, when the shop officer gave me a direct order, I spat in his face and wrecked the shop. I was back in the block, but only while they arranged to ship me out to another prison.

One morning they just came for me and took me to the reception and handcuffed me. They didn't tell me where I was going. Neither I nor my family or next of kin would know my whereabouts until I actually arrived.

Leaving school had been a happy event, but also a traumatic experience. School had never prepared me for the real world outside – it was hard enough just being a human being, but people would insist on making the colour of my skin a bad mark against me before I'd even opened my mouth. Looking back, maybe I should have realised the real world would be like that. After all, if they can give out books in school entitled *Little Black Sambo* and *Little Nigger Boy*, I should have been suspicious from the off about the world outside our classroom walls. As a child you experience being called names, and of course it hurts because you come to realise you're different from the majority and that your people are from the jungle – or so you're always being told; but if you stick up for yourself you usually get left alone until someone else starts again. For the most part it doesn't drastically affect your physical comings and goings, even though mentally it leaves its scars.

I remember being eleven years old when I was living in Bexhill, Sussex. It was wonderful. All the spare time I got I went fishing and sightseeing for weird and wonderful birds and animals. I remember where we lived – it was green with thick foliage smelling of the forest and damp earth. It was a lovely place for a young boy to be. I chased squirrels and even had a tame robin that would follow me about and start singing when it saw me. Yes, those were very happy days, and some of the people there were marvellous to me. Then one day someone called me a 'black wog'. I asked my friend what it meant and he said, 'You're not the same as us, you're a blackie, and my Dad says I shouldn't play with you.' I cried all the way home and now, whenever I think about Sussex, that is what I remember.

There are good people of all races – I do know that now – but when you are young you feel the whole world is against you.

The trouble is that in the outside world you're physically barred from places, denied opportunities, denied jobs, just simply on the strength of your colour. People see you coming, they hold their pockets, clutch their bags to their bosoms. You get on the train and people get up as you sit down; or if the train is packed you find yourself with three spare seats next to you and no one will sit there, they all stand, avoiding your eyes, until some way-out hippy sits down next to you and says, 'Hey man, can I bum a fag off you?' Not only is it embarrassing but highly degrading to treat people in this way. It leaves a sour taste in your mouth and reinforces in your mind the feeling that you are not really part of this society; and so in turn you yourself do not wish to be part of society and this is where the alienation sets in.

My friend Dave and I, both seventeen at the time, once went into a shop in Edgware Road, walked up to the counter and asked for a pack of cigarettes. The man looked us in the face and said, 'I don't serve black people in this shop.' 'All right,' said Dave, 'serve us outside the shop.' The man refused to serve us outside or inside and made it clear we should leave. I suppose the right thing may have been to leave his shop and go elsewhere, but that was impossible for us to – we were proud and headstrong young men. Besides, had we left we would have both been ashamed of ourselves for not standing up for what we knew to be right. We refused to leave and sat down on the floor. The police were called and even though we explained our case we were arrested. Though the shopkeeper may not be typical of shopkeepers in England, his attitude helps to alienate and drive a wedge between the races, and the media helps by reinforcing his prejudices. The mere fact that he was not also arrested only confirmed further to myself and Dave that this society would not look after our welfare, and we decided that if that ever happened again we'd take the law into our own hands and burn the person's shop down. It's not so much the incidents that happen, but society's response to them that leaves a lot of the young generation with no faith in society and its laws. We see society doesn't care what happens to us and we therefore feel the only way is to take matters into our own hands.

One thing we can safely say is that black people will be here for as long as anyone else. So what are we to do about the dilemma of us all living together? What are we to do about our prejudices towards one another? Are we going to try and stop our sons and daughters going out with one another? The world is changing and many of the young of today, regardless of race or creed, are beginning to demand a better and fairer way of life for all. The truth cannot be hidden, and is beginning to come out. The white world has been fooled, lied to and deceived by those in power for too long. It's not a matter of black or white, for we are all human beings, its a matter of good against evil. If you look around the world you can see such troubles, such pain and suffering – yet man has the power to alleviate all this if he so wishes.

Colour is just a distraction, an element of confusion thrown into the melting pot. When we were young as black guys we used to say white people were aliens and came from the skies, because their history is shorter than ours. They don't care about the earth, they killed anything that moved, animals and humans, anything that moved, they killed it. Then they built bombs that can blow up the whole world, and spaceships to go back were they came from, somewhere in the sky. That is why they don't care for this planet, that is why people mean nothing to them, why human misery means nothing to them. This is what we used to say as young guys when taunted about being black and coming from the jungle, but there is an element of truth there, because our earth is being destroyed by man taking anything he can get his hands on by hook or by crook, and pretending that this is the right way to go about things.

Those in power must be stupid or evil if they can't get themselves together and straighten this world out – I've seen five-year-olds co-operating together better than they do.

I truly understand the problem that faces a lot of white people as it gradually begins to dawn on them that black people are not really inferior but as good or bad as anybody else. It must be hard to come to terms with this after hundreds of years being fed a steady diet of lies and untruths that degrade a race of fellow human beings. But no matter how long the papers and television abuse black people, let me tell you, it will never, ever work. Times are changing and the truth will come out; people – not black people, not white people, but *people*, will join together to make this our planet safe for all. *Good on you Bob Geldof*.

Chapter Six

As the van pulled up outside the massive gates I knew we had arrived at Wandsworth. Whether I would be staying for long I wasn't sure, but I knew that I would be here for at least a few weeks. Wandsworth has a reputation throughout the prison system for unpleasantness. Its whole regime is in fact geared to that end so that it can serve as a punishment prison to which prisoners are sent from all over the southern region.

I was passed through the reception, then taken to the block, where I was told I would be seeing the governor in the morning. I was so tired I lay down on the bed and slept without changing. During the governor's round in the morning he stopped off at my cell and told me in no uncertain terms that my unruly behaviour wouldn't be tolerated in his prison, and that as for spitting at his officers, any such act would be dealt with by physical violence to my person. Throughout this tirade I looked straight in his eyes, but when he referred to physical violence to my person I looked at the burly screws who were with him and at the ones who stood at the sides of my door. They were definitely not smiling: I knew they would carry out the governor's threat and probably enjoy it. When he had finished I began to talk both calmly and politely, saying that if a prison like Albany practised racial bias by filling the worst shops in the prison with black inmates without much chance of getting out, then there was bound to be friction. While still in mid-sentence the door was slammed in my face and the governor carried on his rounds. I stayed in the block for another week before being put back into the main wing.

The sewing of mailbags is always associated with prison but so far during my sentence I had not seen one, much less sewn one. Here in Wandsworth everybody sewed mailbags. I was given a long thick needle and some heavily waxed thick black thread that looked like laces from someone's shoes and along with the rest of new starters I was shown how to sew mailbags. We sat in rows sewing and were not allowed to talk or smoke while working. A screw sat in a kind of pulpit-like box that was raised several feet in the air, and if you had any query or question you raised your hand – and that included asking to go to the toilet. The three weeks that I spent there were some of the most depressing of my whole life. There was never any sign of people being at ease, everyone looked so dejected.

The small transistor radio I had was now broken, and with it my one comfort, my one reminder that there was a different world outside these prison walls was gone. The days seemed endless and I lapsed into a dreamy state, not knowing whether I was coming or going or what the time was or what day of the week it was. Any lessons that I could have learned from being in prison had long since been lost, only to be replaced by a deep bitterness that reached the depths of my toes. If prison was supposed to rehabilitate me, then I reasoned that after the first year they should have released me and I would have had a chance of being what they called a 'good citizen'. During that first year I had come to realise that crime wasn't really what I wanted, and that in any case committing a crime for eight thousand pounds was certainly not worth a year or even two months of my life. Had they let me out after a year I would have probably got an honest job, if possible, but whatever I did would have to have been legal. But as time wore on anger was followed by frustration and bitterness at everyone and everything around me.

With so much time on your hands your mind starts to range far and wide – it's the only part of you that can sometimes reach beyond the prison walls – and you wonder if you're living in fantasy or reality. Then the line between sanity and insanity once again becomes very thin indeed. Nearly two years on my whole attitude had changed. The daily conversation between inmates was of a highly political nature. While not being especially articulate, it nevertheless had direction, and was usually aimed squarely at the government. Having achieved some political awareness already, my outlook now focused on the struggle of the white working class. My political ideology had centred on black awareness and the struggle for identity and self determination – and of course I had taken into account the plight of the Third World those whom I recognised as fellow strugglers in South America and Asia, brothers in the cause against imperialism and colonialism. But I now saw a different struggle, an internal struggle between classes in this society, a struggle between the ruling classes and the workers.

My mind turned to the penal institution and how it was riddled with racism. It was an extension of our society but a part that was locked away, hidden by D-notices and Home Office red tape. I realised that this was also a class struggle for black people because what we needed was recognition of our value as people. Our aspirations began with a desire for acknowledgement of our input into society and the world in general, and of the cultural part played by our ancestors in shaping man's history. Ours was a struggle to shake off the shackles of slavery both physical and mental, and it was directed against the colonial mentality of capitalism, which in the schools, in the media and in government sought to brainwash people into believing that we were still pickaninnies, still inferior citizens, wogs and coons who deprived the ruling white society of its full and rightful share. Ours was a struggle for our manhood and womanhood, which involved continually being cornered into proving we were as good as the next person even if we didn't have the same colour skin. Ours was a fight to become aware of who we were as black people in a white country which looked down on us. Ours was the struggle of a colonised people trying to break the bonds of colonialism and the stigma that was attached to a colonised people.

The working class spend most of their lives in debt to banks, finance houses and other such organisations monopolised by the ruling class, and if they aren't in debt for this then they are in debt for that. They too are exposed to the advertising of sleek commercial products, and the telly programmes that portray all the finer things in life that one should aspire to but can never in a million years achieve. Children watch their parents scrimp and save all their lives just for people to knock on the door for payment for some item taken on hire-purchase. The working class work every day just to survive, with no way out of their boring jobs, no prospects or future, while the ruling class have an over-abundance to share among themselves. The working class listen as politicians appear on their telly screens telling lies about the economy and squabbling with each other at every opportunity. It hadn't occurred to me that white people could be disillusioned with the running of their country or unhappy about the unequal distribution of wealth. I had been so wrapped up in my struggle, the black struggle, that I had been in danger of overlooking the internal political struggle taking place in this country. Didn't the struggle of the working class have much in common with our struggle, the black struggle?

I began to look more closely at situations concerning black people and white people's reaction to them and found that I had to re-evaluate my views and re-analyse those situations. For example, the people always demonstrating outside South Africa House were predominantly white. These anti-apartheid campaigners, demonstrating against the treatment of black South Africans, got arrested, went to court, and in many cases were sent to prison. When groups like the National Front marched against black people, again they were confronted by these same white people with their own counter-demonstrations and with the same prison threat hanging over their heads. In my earlier assessments and analyses, I had concluded that these people had their own axes to grind against the government, that they were highly committed to overthrowing the government by any means they could, and I believed them to be controlled and incited by agents provocateurs. Besides, I also felt deeply hurt and ashamed that these white people were out there doing what we should have been doing and in many ways I belittled their efforts through my subconscious shame that we as black people had not organised ourselves and were not politically aware enough to have our own demonstrations. It seemed to reinforce the old lies that black people can't do anything for themselves. It didn't ever really cross my mind seriously that these people might actually believe in what they were doing, that they might actually abhor apartheid and find it disgusting and degrading to fellow human beings. In fact, I didn't really associate them with any kind of political awareness and consciousness. Political knowledge, yes! But political awareness and consciousness, no! I think the reason why I would never acknowledge them to be politically conscious – as I would, say, the Latin Americans – was because of the situation facing black people here in Britain. In the struggle here, black people had not really aligned themselves to any white political group because their understanding of our problems seemed to be different from our own, and in general I felt they were not aware enough of our grievances. Besides, they always wanted to win us over with inducements of financial help. What that really meant was that they would then be able to dictate and control, because we as black people had not yet learned to pool our resources nor recognise our political and economic power.

In my re-evaluation, I saw now that the white protesters had at least reached the first step to becoming conscious: they were upset and embarrassed, and knew that South Africa was wrong; they had reached the first hurdle of being disgusted by the *physical* nature of South Africa, and I hoped that later on they would also come to be more conscious and aware of the mental side of racialism. They lived right in the midst of a racialism that was so overpowering that if they were really conscious they would have been able to see it and would cry tears of shame for subjecting black people to such shame and humiliation. If they could, they would have razed to the ground all the imperialist and bureaucratic symbols in this country that have spread so much evil. There was an obvious contradiction in their demonstrating against apartheid in South Africa, yet failing, or perhaps being unwilling, to recognise the mental anguish caused by racism to black people in their own society. But I acknowledged that we too had our own blind spots and I recognised the importance of the white struggle to change their government's mind about economic involvement in South Africa. They were struggling for change, for a brighter future, because they now came to see that even their children would be caught up in the madness of a world ruled by warmongers who only exploited; and I appreciated that both black and white could in this respect stand united in their quest for a better and more peaceful world for all.

My new-found tolerance and recognition of other people's part in the struggle were strongly reinforced by the genuine disgust shown by my white fellow prisoners at atrocities such as those taking place in South Africa and the plight of disadvantaged peoples generally. Although it may be hard to believe for people who haven't experienced it at first hand, prisoners have strict morals and principles which, unlike a large proportion of society, they stick to. One of the unwritten moral codes is that you help your own, and if you've got and someone else hasn't and they ask, you give or you lend, whether it be tobacco, toothpaste, a book, advice, or just putting someone straight who may be down or depressed. These things may seem minor, but in the context of the bleak existence inside they take on considerable significance. Despite my experiences at Albany, I found that this sense of oppression broke down a lot of the barriers of racism. It was how you acquitted yourself that mattered, not the colour of your skin. I've lost count of the numerous times people banded together to protest at a liberty being taken against a prisoner by the authorities, regardless of whether that person was black or white. So long as he was one of our own, we all grouped together in a show of solidarity. Many white prisoners lost their remission by sticking up for black prisoners who they felt to be right, whether they knew them or not; and the same applied the other way.

In Albany there was an inmate convicted of armed robbery who hadn't been in prison long and didn't like black people at all – in fact he didn't speak to black people and would just walk past you. He was one of the faces and amongst the little firm he was with he commanded a lot of respect. I was just coming up from dinner one day when I saw him standing with a water jug in his hand, his path barred by two screws who were telling him he couldn't go to the recess and get some water; to which he countered that he would not bang up until he got some water as it was a reasonable request Here we go again, I thought, as I sized up the situation.

'Let him have some water, governor,' I said, 'it'll only take him a second.'

I was promptly told by the inmate to mind my own business, 'It's nothing to do with you,' and the look he gave when he said it would have frozen the water itself.

'Get in your cell, Hercules, that's a direct order,' said the screw.

I shrugged my shoulders to both inmate and screw and watched the Mexican stand-off. The inmate then went into a torrent of abuse – 'You slags!' – and questioned the screw's sexuality, calling him a poof. The bell rang and screws ran up the stairs in a great sea of blue and without hesitation bundled us towards the block as other prisoners began to kick and bang their doors with anything they could find.

In these situations you don't have time to be frightened or think about it. Several screws were holding me and one tried to knee me in my crutch so I butted him in the face. One or two had now pulled their truncheons and were steaming into me when the principal officer came up and told them to cool it. The other inmate was more or less in the same position as me – he too had steamed in. Anyway, we managed to get to the block without getting bashed too badly and were both charged with assault. He came out of the block about a week before me, and still passed me on the wing without saying anything to me, nor me to him. But a week later he pushed my cell door open. Then he produced a thermos flask and told me to pass him my cup. 'No tea for me,' I said. 'Pass your cup,' he repeated, 'you'll like this.' He then proceeded to fill my cup full of brandy. We began to drink and got merrier and merrier, soon he disappeared, only to return with a refilled flask. A few of his friends put their heads in the door to see what was happening and I noticed mild surprise on their faces at what they saw; but they were soon sent packing as he told them he was having a nice time with his pal Trevor. It was a really good experience. Here we were, white and black from two different cultures, both suspicious of each other in many ways, but overcoming that to realise we were both human beings.

We talked about when we were young and how our own groups had fought against each other, black against white and white against black; and even though we reckoned we had some nice rows and rucks against each other, we both agreed that if we had been more aware we would have realised it was a lot of bollocks and we would both have been better off firmed up against the system. He explained that he had a misconception about black people and thought they were all mugs and couldn't be trusted; but he did concede that he didn't know many black people and most of what he learned about them came from the telly. We had now finished our tête-à-tête and both his friends and my friends congregated in my cell, talking and reminiscing about days gone by. Even Tommy, the blond-haired bodybuilder who had wanted to start rowing with me when I first arrived, was there. We all talked about our road to prison and if I hadn't really known about crime before I came in, I certainly did now. We got a tremendous kick out of the stunned admiration that greeted us when we told how we had held up security vans with nothing but our bare hands – just grabbing the bags and running off in our naive desperation, with no car and no plan. As the evening wore on it became clear that they no longer saw us as mugs. We were all brought up here, even if not all of us were born in this country. We were a new generation of black people, we knew all about things that were out of order, and even though we could lapse into our patois, we spoke their language just as well if not better than some of them could. If they were white villains then we were black villains. Even if we still had trouble getting our identity accepted outside, here we had earned respect.

Chapter Seven

I was now sent on from Wandsworth and was told I would be going to Gartree prison. Gartree is a maximum-security prison near Leicester, and no different from the rest of the maximum-security prisons. As we passed through the gates I could have been in Albany; the only difference was that here things were not so electronic.

As I settled in I was afforded due respect and courtesy from the boys, white as well as black: shampoo, toothpaste and snouts were presented to me and I was well looked after and wanted for nothing that the inmates could provide. People came and paid their respects, asking about friends of theirs who were in Albany or Wandsworth, and I duly informed them of all the news, or at least as much as I could remember. A white guy who was called the Captain and who carried a lot of swing said they were playing football the next day and did I want to play. Because of my previous experiences playing football in prison, I declined. I thought it best to suss things out and get myself together before I involved myself in anything that could lead to trouble.

I met a couple of guys with whom I had been on remand

and I was happy to see my friend Bigger. He really was big and looked a bit like Mohammed Ali – he had a habit of just smiling and saying 'Cool, man,' when told of the resemblance.

My reputation had preceded me, as I discovered when sitting in the assistant governor's office. 'We have heard a lot about you, Hercules, but we won't tolerate any of your bad behaviour here.' We looked at each other across the table and I took an instant dislike to this man, and I'm sure the feeling was mutual. 'As long as you leave me alone, I'll leave you alone,' I said. This prison was little different from Albany or Wandsworth. Not all the screws were intent on pushing you, but here they had their heavy mob, usually referred to as 'dogs' by the prisoners.

There was one particular screw who homed in on me on some silly pretext whenever he saw me. 'Where you going?' 'What you doing?' 'You're not allowed to have that in your cell.' I usually managed to shake him off when he approached me, but he had taken it as a sign of weakness and was now asking me about a pair of trousers I was wearing that had been bleached. Most of the guys had bleached jeans; he wanted to know how it was that I had managed to get a pair of bleached jeans so soon after arriving.

'Because I'm a black villain,' I said.

'You're no villain, you're a mug.'

'No,' I said, 'I'm not a mug, your mama's a mug.'

He then pointed his finger at my nose, telling me this and that about what he could do to me. I slapped his hand away from my face and he tried to punch me, so I steamed in on him. When the bell went screws came from everywhere with sticks drawn ready to do me, but the rest of the prisoners around me warned them that if they touched me they'd have to deal with all of us. They weren't helped by me, now screaming like a demented man, telling the rest of the screws to come on and hurling abuse at them. I was finally calmed down by Bigger and the Captain, who had to call other prisoners to physically restrain me until I told them I was OK. The Captain and Bigger warned the screws that if anything happened to me there would be a lot of trouble in the prison that night. The next morning I was charged with assault and abusive language. I explained that I had slapped his hand, but that he had tried to punch me first and all I had done was defend myself, which wasn't strictly true but then the screw had already told lies that were beyond belief. He said he had asked me about my jeans and I had immediately set about him. The outcome was that I was remanded in the block to see the Board of Visitors – a panel of outside magistrates and lay-people who could take large chunks of your remission in one go.

A month later I was tried by the Board of Visitors and lost several months remission, with a further twenty-eight days in the block. While in the block I was called for a visit. Surprise surprise, it turned out to be the lovely Dolly. She had come up to see me and as usual she looked like an angel, but the visit took a turn for the worse when she said 'Trevor, try to behave yourself or else they'll keep you in for the whole seven years.' At this I got mad and began telling her through clenched teeth to go and tell the governor and his screws to leave me. Dolly went to get some tea and asked a screw what time the visits finished. When she came back I asked her what she had said to the screw and when she told me, I just stood up and told her to get up and go. 'When you come to see me you never talk to these filth, these people make our lives a misery, these same people take my remission and make my life hell. I'm your man and after all these things they do to me you're fraternising with the enemy. Please don't come and see me again, I want a woman who's gonna stick by her man and not fraternise with my enemy.' She began to cry saying, 'You've changed, you've changed.' I turned and left.

I was now becoming an animal in a caged environment where I couldn't get out, and the baiting and taunting of the keepers made me more and more angry. Even after I was up from the block the situation remained the same. During the feast of Ramadan, a Moslem time of fasting, they were sending up pork, for our evening meals and we protested. The inevitable happened: I was back in the block again.

They took so many liberties that at times the whole prison refused to eat the food which was left on the hot plate – not a single prisoner came down for the meals. The screws became heavy-handed, putting people on report for nothing at all. Every day you were stopped and searched though as I learned from other prisoners, this had been going on for at least a year before I arrived and was steadily pushing nerves to breaking point. Strikes were organised, with everyone refusing to go to work. But the main complaint was against the medical staff, who could be seen dragging people off never to be seen again. The doctor was a joke. For any ailment you had he gave you aspirin and water, and you couldn't complain because you were immediately ushered out of the room. If you caused too much trouble you went on the missing list, only to turn up in the hospital drugged up to the eyeballs with Largactil, Depixol or some other zombifying drug.

About this time I was suffering from tonsillitis, but would not go to the doctor even though I couldn't open my mouth and was so sick and weak that I could eat nothing. I finally collapsed and my friends took me to the hospital. They arranged for the red band who cleared the hospital to send a report back to my friends every day so they could make sure nothing untoward happened to me. This was very important in Gartree, where others who had been in the hospital suddenly vanished, only to reappear in Broadmoor. Finally I was sent to Wormwood Scrubs, which has a hospital wing where they do operations. Of course I was very dubious, but when I arrived in the hospital the nurses were so kind and professional that I soon felt at ease – one particular Irish nurse was especially nice. I settled down and even found a long-lost friend, Boxer Johnny. When we hugged each other in the middle of the ward you could see that people were genuinely happy that we had found each other. We both agreed that life was a bitch but in the hospital ward there were no screws, only nurses; the occasional male nurse would come in but soon leave. The atmosphere was like a breath of fresh air to us prisoners, who were used to living under a much more oppressive routine. It was almost like being in a real hospital, except that now and again a screw would pop his head round the door to look in. The nurses on duty during the day usually changed shift with other nurses about six in the evening, and they would stay until the morning shift arrived.

I hadn't been with a women in years and the sight of those nurses running around in their lovely tight uniforms made my blood boil, so you can imagine my delight when one night I saw a pretty black nurse reporting for duty. My immediate thought was, 'T, try a t'ing.' I engaged her in conversation and though she was eager to talk to me I couldn't see myself getting anywhere. Box Johnny was watching my progress and as his bed was opposite mine he had a very clear view of my chat-up technique. At the most inopportune times he would come over and join in, but I tried my best to get rid of him because by this time I had got the conversation round to some nice intimate sexual chat, telling her how I hadn't had a woman for years and so on. Then Johnny came over yet again, talking some mundane rubbish, and she got bored and moved off.

One night when she was on duty and checking the patients, who I believed to be all asleep, I called her over feigning pain in my stomach while making the appropriate hushed groans.

'What's wrong, Trevor?'

'I've got these pains in my stomach and lumps come up.'

I think she genuinely believed me but she was in for a surprise.

'Where does it hurt?' she said as she now stood over me.

I took her hand and put it under the blanket onto the erection that I now had. She made a token gesture of removing her hand, but then gradually began to move her hand up and down my erection, and believe me, it was heaven. Then I heard 'A you dat, Trevor.' There was Boxer Johnny, sitting up in bed and peering at both of us. He still doesn't understand why I refused to talk to him for three days after that. No matter how I tried, I could never get her to give me any more handouts.

The operation was successful and I was soon back in Gartree, where I walked straight into a protest about the medical treatment. A prisoner had been sent to Broadmoor and the prisoners were up in arms, but it soon died down. I continued to get myself into trouble and the block became my second home.

I had decided early on during my sentence that I wouldn't have any kind of luxuries in my cell – no curtains, bedspread, pieces of carpet or nick-nacks. My cell was bare and I thought to keep it that way so I wouldn't get too comfortable. The last thing I wanted was to become conditioned to this way of life to the point where I didn't think or do for myself and just became a robot programmed by the screws. I had now stopped writing any letters – I had never written many anyway, maybe four every six months – and all my letters and personal things I had I destroyed, much to the annoyance of the screws who got a great kick out of going through prisoners' personal belongings. It gave the screws a feeling of power over you to sift through the most intimate things we owned, such as pictures of family and loved ones. I wasn't going to give them the satisfaction.

I could not bring myself to write to Dolly because of the personal nature of the letters. Not that I wished to apologise

– I didn't. I firmly believed I was right, and that as my woman she was a part of me, a part of the struggle. As a black woman her allegiance should have been one hundred per cent behind me; how could she have even contemplated talking to a screw when she knew what I and most of the black people in these places had been through. Even some of her own family had been through the same racist prison system. Anyway, I was glad she was not coming any more – less pressure on me. I reasoned that the struggle for survival in this country for black people was the same for both men and women, but that we sometimes veered in different directions, to fight a different part of that battle. I believed that women didn't fully understand men and vice versa, and the more and more we men talked about women the more we believed that. Here we were in prison and out of fifty or so men who all claimed to have had women before we came in, only three got visits from them. Even in the case of the married ones, their wives had sought divorce. Many a time we sat and watched as the white prisoners' wives and girlfriends came up regularly, while we were lucky to receive one letter a year. It was very depressing. Only when you're in a position of confinement in a penal institution can you really imagine the joy of receiving a letter, the way it lifts you up and rejuvenates you to cope with the pressures inside.

The extent of racism directed towards the black male in this society at times is very hard for our women to comprehend. As far as white society is concerned, the black male represents a threat to his white supremacy and all that it stands for, because we have shattered their age-old lie that they are a superior race. Just as they cling to the idea of empire, they cling to the threads of shattered myths. Now we, especially the young, see them for what they are and the fear and respect our parents afforded them is not and never will be forthcoming from us. As far as we are concerned, people have to earn respect. They always say that black men are violent, but what could be more violent than nuclear weaponry – all controlled by white governments.

Most whites still cling to their superiority myth and any black male who refutes that attracts trouble in the form of degradation, threats, intimidation verbal abuse, physical abuse, and finally prison. To walk on the street is itself an experience in the art of survival for the black male, never mind driving a car. But if you have a lady with you it's not so bad; they seem to think you represent less of a threat, and also there's a chance that a woman may be believed in a court of law. How many times have we as black men heard, 'Where are you going? What have you got in your pockets? Where are the drugs, then? Where did you get this money?' And then comes the indignity of being searched in the street as people pass by watching the by now familiar scene. How many times has a police car driven by with the occupants shouting out 'Black bastards!' The public have been so brainwashed that the sight of a few black males passing is enough for them to ring the police to say that they've seen suspicious looking black people walking by. The amount of black men in prison for assault on police has to be seen to be believed – people who protested at being harassed on the street for nothing, and were then thrown in a police van and assaulted by the police, only to be charged themselves with assault. Charge any black man and the chances are he will be convicted. Driving your car can be a nasty experience: 'Is this your car? Where did you get it?' They search your car and give you a producer (to take your documents to a police station). Five producers in a week is not uncommon.

If you walk into any building people immediately come up to check you out: 'Can I help you? Do you want someone here?' It doesn't matter where you are, there's continual pressure on your head because in this society the black male is seen as a threat. The black male in turn has acquired his own responses, like 'Fuck off!', because the continual pressure eventually leads to frustration. It's hard enough being a human being without people bringing the black element into it – and when they do the next thing you know you're charged with some nonsense because some racist has confronted you with some rubbish and you've taken the bait. The struggle for black men to establish their true identity and manhood seems never-ending, and the only time they can relax is at home with their women.

Is the struggle any easier for women? This society does see them as less of a threat, especially physically. As far as jobs and suchlike go, they're far more likely to be able to attain high positions, as long as they don't wear locks or wraps on their heads which to this society would represent a threat because it shows awareness of their roots. The black woman will be on first-name terms with the boss, go to the pub with work-mates because she is far more readily accepted by this society – especially if the boss and other white male workers have designs to get her into the nearest bed. Therefore the treatment a black woman receives from society is different in many ways – it tends to help her become more integrated. The treatment we as black males receive on the other hand, distils in us an even more fervent desire not to be part of this society.

I hasten to add that I'm rather generalising. Women have their own difficulties and pressures concerning the bringing-up of their children, at times on their own when they have to be both mother and breadwinner. I thought about Dolly and knew that a man's attitude to the screw would have been the same as mine. I decided to contact Dolly and try and talk and discuss things with her, so I put a visiting order in an envelope and sent it to her, though without a letter as I wasn't prepared to share my thoughts with the screw who would be censoring the mail.

The subject of black relationships has been something that

has been hiding away in our subconscious, not to be talked about. Well, now we're going to talk about it. As I've said already, there's no point in hiding away and cheating ourselves. If we're searching for the truth we have to bring things out into the open where we can challenge their authenticity, even if it means searching the very depths of our souls, bringing anguish and pain in an endeavour to put things right. Let's get away from macho bullshit. There's no shame or embarrassment in having messed up in your relationships or in your responsibilities towards those you love. The real sign of a man or woman is being able to rectify your mistakes. Everybody messes up, but if you face the truth of your failure and do nothing about it, then you've really failed.

If relationships between black people is a subject that has not been openly discussed, this is largely the fault of male machismo and egotism. Man is the dominant force in the world, or rather controls the world, and has put woman on a pedestal as a secondary thing, beautiful, attractive, accepted them as a partner, but not on an equal basis. It's quite handy for men to be in control of their relationships, and also in control of their responsibilities in those relationships. We as black men have fallen into a trap: our dominance of the world is a fake, it is dominance without any real power; so we place our women on pedestals, to be dominated in order for us to feel we are real men, part of that dominant force of the world. But as black men we don't control the world, we're not the dominant force and there's no need to swagger about as if we do, swelling up our chests and being macho, talking loud in the dark and saying nothing. We don't need to live a lie and be fakes. We don't need to prove our manliness by sexing anything that moves in a skirt. We don't need to prove our courage like fighting cocks in an endeavour to say, 'Heh! I'm brave, I'm strong, I'm bad.'

No, what we want are men who will take charge of their responsibilities – that's being a man, that's being dominant if you like. Carry out your duties as a man and don't duck issues, face up to real life, not some macho bullshit dream. We need strong relationships, built on sincerity and responsibility. We need relationships, built on the mental and emotional as well as the physical. We need time to get to know more about each other than just our physical attributes. If you want love to be no more than a black buck needing a wench and the wench needing a pickaninny, then go ahead, regress back to slavery! If your black male ego needs to be fulfilled, then I suggest you find some other way of fulfilling it, without hurting someone else's feelings without proving your machismo by begetting a child that you then fail to take responsibility for because your machismo is false, it has disappeared in a whiff of fake dominance when confronted by the real business of being a man.

You may feel you're the only one and at times you may feel like a child of the night, lost in a cocoon of emptiness, deprived of love from your family or those close to you. But let me assure you, you are not alone in that feeling of emptiness, of being wronged and unloved by those you feel should love you. Most black people here and their families don't have normal relationships because it's been a struggle to survive, and in that struggle a lot of us have become insensitive and consumed with our own wellbeing and our own goals. This struggle to survive has made our lives precarious and unbalanced, so that we don't have time to relate to each other, we have become selfish and uncaring in the pursuit of our 'thing' as it were, so self-absorbed that we rarely have time to give ourselves to others. Whether it be your family, your loved ones, or your friends, there always seems to be something missing. People don't seem to have time to give part of themselves, they won't wait for things to develop and take their natural course. We're for ever pushing our relationships for an answer straight away, so no wonder we never get the answer we want and are always moving on in pursuit of something else. No wonder we end up feeling like an empty shell, a hard outer case, a shield that's nigh on impregnable to someone else trying to get through to you emotionally, even though their intentions may be honourable and good. You may give yourself physically, but your inner self, your emotions your feelings, you keep under wraps, you fear to let them out in the open where they can get hurt by someone who just moves on, leaving even deeper scars than the ones you already have. But deep down you know you're destroying and hurting yourself even more. Deep down is a well of emotions, feelings and love waiting to be drawn upon for your body to feel free, and you injure your spirit by not drawing upon this well because the water of your love becomes stale, stagnant and undrinkable.

When love has welled up inside of women and needs to be released they have babies who they can lavish their affection on. But us men, we seem to turn to aggression in our frustration, because to let so much pent-up emotion out in one go would make men feel vulnerable and weak and soft – what a blow to their machismo, ego, and most of all to their fake dominance! The ever-increasing call in this society to put yourself first, pursue your own goal, do your own thing, go off on your own, be an individual – this can only cause distress to the black community because the less you give your time to others, the more lonely and isolated you become and we need the support and love of our brothers and sisters more than most. Relationships need to be worked on and cultivated before they will blossom and flower. Not only does it take time, it takes patience and energy; it takes you, not just a part of you, but *all* of you.

Materialism seems to play a large part in the lives of black people, at times even at the cost of their own families. We seem to feel that the dedicated, blinkered all-consuming quest for the acquisition of wealth somehow compensates for the lack of something in our lives. Materialism consumes us more than other people. We as black people are always having to prove ourselves because of the colour of our skin, we have to be twice as good as the next man to achieve the same position. We're the social outcasts of society, with no real economic muscle, and so we see the acquisition of wealth as our way out. It offers status in a society that is based on materialism, wealth, gold, diamonds, big flash cars, big houses with swimming pools, fine clothes. People in this society *kill* for things like that, *go to war* for things like that, so is it any wonder that we as black people now adopt that thirst for personal wealth? As black people we think we can wrap ourselves in a cocoon of wealth and be safe and warm away from the nasty things in the world, the hurtful things, the taunts, the racism that so affects our lives that we're willing to go out and risk our own freedom in the pursuit of this wealth. In fact a lot of black people believe that money transcends the colour barrier and gives them the things that they crave most – respect, and status, but most of all equality. If it doesn't bring these things, then they hope at least to make life as comfortable and as bearable as possible. When you acquire wealth, rightly or wrongly, you believe you are somebody, and it's true that society also regards the rich as somehow more important than the poor. Who cares where it came from as long as you don't get caught stealing it? So men and women do all manner of evil, even to the extent of selling their souls for this thing called wealth that can make you 'somebody', but the endeavour to climb up the social and economic ladder simply hardens them and blinds them to their real needs. Ninety-nine per cent of them won't even make it up that ladder; they will be left at the roadside, embittered, frustrated and mostly incapable of proper or decent relationships. The good things within them, their honesty and their capacity to love, they traded in for their all-consuming desire for wealth.

The family unit is the backbone of any people, yet we black people here have failed in that department. Our relationships with our parents have left a lot of us with a sour taste and a bad feeling, and many of us still suffer mentally as a result of the wrongs we believe were done to us. Even now, we may still find it hard to forgive. Many people out there can tell a story of family pain, so don't feel you're alone. People remember being thrown out at a young age; people still show the scars of heavy beatings; people still show the scars of being left on their own in the house too long; people remain bitter about wickednesses committed by members of their extended families. It is the age-old clash of young against old. But now is the time to forget all the wrongs you feel have been done to you, stop brooding, feeling sorry for yourself, because these things can no longer be used as excuses. We've all been through it but we must learn to overcome it so we can teach our children with love, warmth and understanding.

If you look inside yourself you know that if you have any responsibilities and don't live up to them, then you're not a man. It is not macho to run away from what you know you should do, and no one will respect you for not even trying to do your duty. Anyone can fuck up, but the mark of a real man is to try and rectify your mistakes.

Those of us who have children have to draw them close. We are the ones to guide and protect them, and show them the way. Not one of you who have children can opt out of your responsibilities, and if you have, start crying because you're a wicked motherfucker. If you're not prepared to give up your life for your child then you shouldn't have gotten any. Your child should come first. I know there's many people out there right now fucking up, but you'd better get your act together because if you don't when those children do grow up they'll loathe and hate you. As a man I don't see many black fathers out with their children, looking after them and just generally being in love with their children in the open. Get out there, man, let's see who you are! Get the children and take them out to the park, to the zoo, any-where. Just get them out, so we can see all those proud fathers who in turn will inspire others.

I had been in nearly four years now, plenty of time to think over issues like this, but mostly I had tried to forget about the outside world. The frustration I and the rest of the black guys felt began to get to us and we all took to locking ourselves in our cells to read and just contemplate life. This state of apathy continued for about three months until I took to going to the gym with one of the guys from the Spaghetti House seige. We worked out a regular routine, took to jogging and altogether got ourselves in shape. What had really prompted this was a game of football, just a 'friendly' on the wing, though it turned out to be anything but that.

A black guy by the name of Giant, who used the gym regularly and who looked like Mr Universe, was in possession of the ball when a small Scottish boy by the name of Jimmy tackled him. I say tackled, but Jimmy had no intention of going for the ball, he just booted Giant with a full, blatant kick. Everyone stopped playing, expecting Giant to steam in straight away because what Jimmy had done was an affront and by the unwritten laws of prison etiquette he was entitled to steam in – everyone would have said he was right. Instead he just stood there looking at Jimmy. The reason for Giant's fear was that little Jimmy was known as a blade-merchant and had cut quite a few people during his prison sentence. He had a bad reputation. He was now abusing Giant in the most embarrassing fashion – black bastard, wog, nigger, and those watching looked at each other with a silent pleading that Giant would steam in. Giant was a physical freak, he couldn't lose, why didn't he get on with it?

Giant was the epitome of what white people would call black power – about six-foot tall and all muscle; I believe he could have lifted up a house if he had wanted to. But we black guys had sussed him out long ago as a coward. Apparently so had Jimmy, and whoever had put Jimmy up to it because Jimmy himself wasn't that way inclined. Quite a few of the white firms hated Giant. He didn't have much to do with us black guys, but was always underneath those white guys' asses, and they adopted him just like some pet. He thought by being with those white firms he was being a gangster. We more or less blanked him, but the humiliation of him on the yard was like a stab at all of us black guys. Here was the biggest, strongest black man being humiliated in the middle of the prison yard, and all the progress we as black people had made in establishing ourselves and gaining respect was now being eroded right in front of our eyes.

'Who you calling a black bastard, you mug?' Before I knew it I had stepped forward. I hadn't consciously done so but here I was now confronting Jimmy.

'I wasn't talking to you, Trevor.'

'What you calling the guy all these black names for then, if you and him want a row then have a row, but don't bring all this black business into it, you cunt.'

'You're always poking your nose in, Hercules, fuck off out of it, you're the mug,' said one of the guys on the sideline who was with a North London firm.

We began to fight but were soon pulled apart. The screws told us all to go in. As we did so, the guy was shouting how he was going to kill me and so on, and when a man in prison tells you he's going to kill you, you have to take it seriously.

As we walked in, Bigger and a few other black guys were saying I should do him as soon as we were inside. They also said that if anyone else started they would all steam in. There was a great feeling of closeness, an experience of solidarity that will last forever. I was in my own world. I knew I was going to do him, and that was that. My life flashed in front of me in a fountain of colour, and as Dolly flashed up a stab of pain hit me, followed by regret that now I might not be able to tell her I was sorry. I had no choice but to fight; even if I wanted to run away I couldn't, but I didn't even want to. I wasn't frightened because the several years I had spent in prison had conditioned me to this kind of inevitable drama. It wasn't even a question of winning or losing, what was important was to come out of it with honour and dignity. Of course I had my blade, as nearly everyone did, and that was the first thing I got when I came into the wing. I was shadowed by two of the black guys as they watched my back, and we were astounded as the guy I was looking for headed into the showers with a towel wrapped around his waist. One of my friends pushed a towel into my hand and whispered, 'Don't blade him, T, do him with this, give me the blade.' I gave it to him and opened the towel to find a large chunk of wood, probably a table leg. I went into the shower and began to set about him. The only thing I really remember was him slipping all over the place and the water showering down on me.

Life carried on in much the same vein, except that I was now a student of the Open University, studying sociology and trying to get my act together. I had been inspired by George Jackson and other black American prisoners who thought education essential. I also felt so myself, and decided to take advantage of the education available. But first I had to stay out of the block long enough, as well as fight hard to get on the course. Much to the disappointment of several screws and one AG, I got on.

The prison continued in a state of unrest, and if people weren't complaining about the food they were complaining about the incompetence of the medical fraternity. Years of frustration coupled with the prison staff attitude of, 'You're a prisoner, that's why,' or 'Because we said so,' or 'You're nicked,' all added fuel to an already simmering volcano.

One particular day my door was opened early in the morning for breakfast, and as is my usual ritual I put the small wedge in my door to make it impossible for anyone outside to push it open more than an inch or so. I turned over and covered my head and endeavoured to get back to sleep as

I didn't want breakfast. After a few minutes something just told me to turn round. It was just the slightest feeling of a presence, and as I turned I saw the same guy I had fought in the showers standing over my bed with a knife. I grabbed his hand and managed to get him to drop the knife just as Bigger appeared in the doorway. We hustled the intruder onto the landing floor where he was helped to his cell. The screws knew something had gone on and I reckoned they would move one of us out of the prison to avoid any further conflict. Two days later he was shipped out. There was no trouble over it as his little firm said to me: 'It's between the two of you – you don't like him and he doesn't like you, you reckon you can do him and he reckons he can do you. As long as no one else interferes, we won't.' And they didn't.

I had now come to the end of my course and all that was really left was the written exam. But the winds of change would see to it that I never took that exam. Trouble was brewing and it was over the medical treatment of a black prisoner. Several prisoners had been committed to Broadmoor from Gartree, and the main talking point amongst the prisoners was that they had been sent merely because they were a nuisance to the system, and not at all because they were crazy. Feeling was running high.

Chapter Eight

Thursday came and with it an event that I never wish to experience again. It was the scariest moment of my life and I honestly didn't believe I would live to see the night out. The previous night, a few of us black guys had congregated in a cell chatting and larking about, and during the horseplay Bigger and another black inmate we named Yardy began a wrestling match that was all in good spirits. That was the cue for the rest of us to jump up and test our strength against each other until we all settled down into various forms of disarray, panting and laughing and trying to catch our breath. In the morning Yardy complained of a pain in his neck due to the previous night's exertions and we urged him to see the doctor – much to his disgust because, as I've said before, the medical treatment at Gartree was a joke. But he relented and put his name down for the sick parade.

Sick parade was a matter of reporting sick early before you went to work. The wing screw would take your name and you would have to wait until about ten o'clock before you saw the doctor, which meant you didn't go to work with the rest of the prisoners but stayed in the wing. Granted, reporting sick could have been used as a way to skive off work for a couple of hours, but we as prisoners never really used it for this purpose. For a start, if you were reported sick you were locked up until such time you saw the doctor, which meant they docked your wages, and believe me a couple of hours away from work could be the difference between you getting tobacco or not on pay day. But the main reason that deterred people from reporting sick was the erratic doctor – or rather the medical orderly screws who most times told the doctor what medicine to administer as if it were some kind of joke. The standard joke amongst them when you reported sick was to issue 'rest in cell', which meant that for the number of days you were given you were locked up in your cell, and the only time your door was opened was when you were handed your food. You were allowed to see and talk to nobody, so it was much the same as being in the block. Rest in cell was ordered for anything from a cut finger to a headache, a pain in your back, toothache – you name the medical complaint, the order was rest in cell. Of course while this was going on you didn't get paid. A lot of people lost plenty of remission for protesting over the issuing of rest in cell, but mainly we feared the medical staff. Those men in white coats could be talking to you one minute, then the next minute you were on the missing list, and wouldn't reappear until they'd made a zombie of you.

One of our friends, Dread, had experienced at first hand what we had now come to refer to as the liquid cosh. Many of us, white as well as black, protested and lost remission over his case – as well as over other cases which involved white prisoners. We nursed Dread through his period of insensibility with encouragement and at times harsh abuse: 'Stand firm, Dread, you weakheart. You don't see how the man mash you up. You a dread, lion, stand firm, Dread.' We even told him we would cut off his locks if he didn't shape up, though we had no intention of doing this and he knew it

– it was just our way of urging him on to greater effort. He was so affected by the drugs that he used to walk exactly like Boris Karloff as Frankenstein's monster. Before the drugs Dread had been a supreme athlete and an outstanding footballer; it was a joy to play alongside him, and he helped earn us the nickname our friends gave us, the black raiders.

We coaxed him back to normality, and after the frustration of nursing him like a baby to see him running around again lifted all our spirits. One day, sitting on the field watching him playing football again, someone produced some rot-gut made from potatoes, yeast and sugar, and we toasted our achievement in looking after our own and striking a blow at the system. It was heartening to know that we had all stood firm, both black and white, over issues that concerned us all, and the wonderful feeling of solidarity taught many of us black guys to look at some of these white guys with a new respect. You could see by the screws' faces they were gutted that white and black had united over the issue.

Soon afterwards, and within weeks of what should have been his eventual release, Dread was suddenly transferred – to where we didn't know, but through the prison grapevine we soon learned he had been taken to Broadmoor. We contacted several black and white organisations by smuggling out letters telling them of Dread's plight and the huge campaign which took off outside finally forced the authorities to release him, once outside independent doctors had revealed there was nothing wrong with the man.

We know why Dread was singled out for this treatment, as some others also were. Firstly, he didn't really have any contact with people outside and didn't receive any letters. He was basically alone, with no one outside making sure he was all right, which is imperative to someone doing a prison sentence because with nobody to turn to and no one keeping an eye on you, the prison authorities see you as fair game for abuse and ill-treatment. Secondly, Dread wore his hair in dreadlocks, and his accent was strongly patois. He was strictly non-violent, always talking about red, gold and green, Jah, going back to Africa, and quoting the Bible to screws who were always nicking him for some trivia. They constantly tried to take the piss out of him with sarcastic innuendoes because his English wasn't that good; he also happened to fit in strongly with the screws' stereotype of black people. To cap it all, as a Rastafarian he campaigned for his religion to be recognised by the prison authorities, claiming that they should provide a proper diet, as they were supposed to for Jews, vegans, Moslems and others. As they knew he didn't eat pork they continually gave it to him and it was an endless struggle for him because they were always behind him, goading him on and then placing him on report.

One of the tricks the screws played was to talk to a black guy about something, then go away and in the morning you'd be nicked. When you read the charge sheet you found you had been nicked for saying something like 'Ras bomber', or some other such concocted bullshit, and you'd actually be found guilty and lose remission. Because of Dread's strong West Indian accent they were always using that to nick him. One day, a few weeks before the fateful Thursday, I was up in front of the governor charged with saying 'Bomber'. When I inquired of the governor what this word meant he told me that it didn't matter what the word meant, he, the governor, had found me guilty of saying it and he took two days remission from me! If I was going to lose my remission it might as well be for something. 'Fuck you, governor.' Another spell in the block followed, but now I refused to see the governor at all when he came on his rounds and my door was opened. Instead I would rant and rage like a madman, telling the governor about his mother, father, sister, and that he was an asshole. The profanity and abuse that came from my lips was straight from the gutter. It got so bad that they didn't even open my door when the governor made his rounds, but I always knew when he was there and would rant and rave, banging my door and shouting and screaming at the top of my voice: 'The governor is a fucking whore, his wife sucks.' He always made his visits as short as possible and I was never nicked once for the abuse I hurled.

The block was now filling up as the atmosphere on the wings became intense and electric; and the now familiar complaint against medical ill-treatment was the main cause. They finally let me up after I had spent an extra seven days there at my own request, because when they had told me I was going back to the wing I was lying on the floor on my coat dozing so I told them to fuck off as I was sleeping and was not ready to leave. I continued to do that for seven days, after which I told them they were all filth and I couldn't care less about being in the block and if they thought they could break me they were mistaken, I was a warrior, a lion, a rasta.

I came out of the block on the Tuesday before Yardy went sick with pain in his neck from wrestling the night before. The day passed uneventfully until the afternoon, when it was discovered that Yardy was missing. Still, nobody really paid a great deal of attention until, an hour before tea-time, a reliable source reported to several of us that Yardy was in hospital where he was in bad shape after being forcibly drugged. As you can imagine, when this news got out things began to boil; as the rest of the prisoners returned from work and greeted the news with the same indignant anger, the tension rose higher and higher. It was now tea-time and we were banged up while the screws went off to have their own tea.

As I sat alone in my cell waiting to be unlocked after finishing my tea, I never dreamed of the kind of impact Yardy's treatment would have upon the rest of the prison population, and also upon myself. I knew the prisoners were angry, as they had a right to be, and as I was myself. But certain things had happened in the prison before to prisoners and although people had spoken out about them, there hadn't yet been a real show of solidarity by the whole prison. I had no reason to believe this episode would be any different – in prison you look after your own, that is one of the golden rules, and you choose your friends very carefully because what they do reflects on you and vice versa. In a situation which involves a friend of yours, whether with the prison authorities or with other prisoners, you stand by him and if anything is to be said or done you have to be the one to say or do it. Other people who see the situation impartially will tell you if you are right or out of order, and it works quite well within the context of prison.

Bigger, myself and one of the guys from the Spaghetti House siege were like spokesmen for our little firm, and if any trouble occurred between one of our firm and anyone else they would usually come to one of us and say that one of our people had been out of order and tell us what had happened. We would then go about trying to patch it up so as to keep things peaceful. If the shoe was on the other foot, we'd go and speak to their spokesmen and they would try and sort out the trouble. That's the way it was and everybody respected that. So, as the situation stood, Yardy was on our firm and we had to be the ones to inquire about his welfare. Even though people felt strongly about it, it was left up to our firm to stick up for him; not that other people wouldn't, but if his friends didn't stick up for him, why should anyone else? Also, if you weren't prepared to stick up for your friends, what kind of respect could you expect to get from the rest of the prisoners? I didn't really know what we could do, but if past experiences, especially Dread's, made me resolute not to be fobbed off with the usual evasions. The ensuing riotous mayhem was not planned in any way, and the solidarity between prisoners that night was the most wonderful advertisement for racial harmony that I have ever experienced. It gives hope to us all that one day we may all be able to live alongside each other on equal terms.

When we were unlocked after tea I came face to face with

Bigger on the landing and without exchanging a single word we both descended the stairs. We both knew what had to be done and I knew that somehow this night would remain with me for the rest of my life. I didn't know what would happen but my spirit, my whole being, told me something would. When we got to the office they were obviously expecting us as there were more than the usual number of screws on duty and two or three stood directly in the doorway, trying to intimidate us from coming in. Bigger went through them like a knife through butter and I followed in his slipstream, sticking close to the big fella. I remember the bright fluorescent light illuminating everything in the office. We were surrounded by screws and it was just as if we were prisoners of war and had been captured and brought in for questioning.

We asked the reason for Yardy being in the hospital and told them that to our knowledge he was being held against his will and had been forcibly drugged. They replied that they didn't know why he was in the hospital, or even if he was in the hospital at all. They finally ended up by telling us that they knew nothing about anything and if we wanted to find out about Yardy we would have to wait until the morning and ask the doctor. This explanation obviously wasn't good enough for us, so Bigger and I told the screws that we would like someone to go over to the hospital to make sure Yardy was OK. They refused. We told them that we weren't happy with that, and demanded that someone should go over to see Yardy. We gave them an ultimatum, both of us now shouting and screaming at everything in a blue uniform, informing them that at seven-thirty, if no one had seen Yardy, we would tear this whole place down, starting with their own office and anyone in it. It was now six-thirty, and as we turned to leave we saw half the wing population gathered outside the office door, all looking very stern and serious and hurling abuse at the screws, saying how the prison would be razed to the ground if Yardy wasn't released and that we wouldn't accept any more people going on the missing list. Everyone was coming up to me and the people on our little firm, saying we had done right and everyone was backing us.

The first inkling I got of the seriousness of the situation was when a few people came up to me with home-made balaclavas and weapons the like of which I had never seen before. Where they had hidden these weapons God only knows. For the first time since being in prison I realised these places were a time bomb. It was the only time in my life I had been really frightened – I shuddered to think that these same weapons could have been turned against me had I been in a row with some of these people. We told people to cool it, explaining that our main concern was to make sure Yardy was all right, that the object of the exercise was to get someone over to see how he was, and that we should all remain calm until seven-thirty. By now the other three wings had got wind of the situation and the whole prison was buzzing with tension. As prisoners we all knew there had to come a time when we would stand up and be counted over the medical ill-treatment of prisoners. We all felt strongly about it and knew that we had to act as one to leave no doubt in the minds of the prison authorities as to how we felt about their abuse of their medical powers.

I wouldn't pretend for one minute that the medical problem was the sole motivation for everybody's anger; but that anger had been brewing for years. Added to that was the frustration of confinement over a long period of time and the constant mental anguish of standing up to the prison ordeal. There was deep resentment and bitterness at a system that many felt should have released them a long time ago, resentment at a system that they found hypocritical, a system that said you were innocent until you were found guilty but could keep you under appalling conditions for several months awaiting trial. Then, when you finally came to court, you could be found not guilty and sent packing without so much as <u>an apology, let </u>alone recompense. We were angry at a system which claimed you were in prison for rehabilitation but which merely contained you in conditions that dehumanised you and turned you into an animal among other animals, conditions under which you had to be macho and have the killer instinct to survive with your dignity intact. We felt bitterness at a system that left you good for nothing else but crime because the education you learned inside was a criminal education. We felt frustration at a parole system that nobody understood and which was used to dupe and fool people into having a false sense of hope and belief, only to leave them disconsolate and dejected when they found the truth that they had been used like a donkey with a carrot on a string dangled before its face. Then there were those who were rotten to the core: whether prison or society had made them that way is debatable but they hated everything and everyone, and had neither political convictions nor ideals nor any form of consciousness. They didn't distinguish one form of trouble from another but relished trouble for its own sake.

At seven o'clock several senior prison officers arrived on our wing, where they were greeted by loud jeers. I somehow found myself as spokesman with the inevitable Bigger at my side, and we were quickly engaged in heated argument with these officers. Behind us stood the whole wing, and whenever we made a point that the prisoners agreed with it was greeted by loud cheers. The officers were obviously uncomfortable and eager to placate us with the usual bullshit of passing the buck onto someone else. They had nothing to do with the situation, they said, but still they pretended they had no power to let one of us go over to the hospital to see Yardy, which was in fact a blatant lie. I had never been in any kind of mass violence before and it was not obvious to me that we were on the verge of a full-blown riot. As far as I knew we were sticking up for what few rights we did have as prisoners, but I'm sure the screws with their training recognised the situation as potentially riotous.

The outcome of the talk with the senior officer was that they agreed to seek permission from higher up for someone to go and see that Yardy was all right. Many people took this as a sign of them backing down to our demands and the mood became somewhat lighter. It was a sign that we as a force, as a unit, had exercised our rights and that the system had been forced to concede to us. At seven-twenty a senior officer whom none of us had seen before was escorted into the wing by several of his henchmen. Where they dug him up from is anybody's guess, but a string of medals hung from his uniform. The utter nonsense and lies that came from this man's lips had to be heard to be believed. He addressed me as if I was a colonial subject just off the boat from Africa or the West Indies, telling me that my friend Yardy had been 'playing up' – as if to say, I know what you boys get up to and for your own good you must be kept apart from normal people until you get over your volatile ways and persecution complex. Unfortunately, continued Medallion Man, there was no way anybody could see Yardy – that would be a matter for the governor to decide in the morning. With that he stood back with a smug smile on his face as if to say, I can mug you off all day.

The troops behind me were obviously and noisily furious and in an instant the man's mood changed as he realised the extent of his miscalculation. He hadn't believed that prisoners would back a black prisoner over what he believed to be a black issue, which to us of course it wasn't. He had even thought he could baffle us with the science of his tongue – after all, we were just prisoners. Well, how wrong he was!

'What time is it?' I asked him. 'Um, seven thirty-five.'

With that I walked into the office and began to smash everything and anything that could be destroyed. Within seconds the whole place was in turmoil. We were in darkness as the lights had been cut off, and the sound of crashing and smashing could be heard all around me. The hot-plate came through the office wall, pinning my leg underneath it and the rubble for a few seconds until I freed myself.

It was off, the whole wing was up in the air. Screaming prisoners raced to and fro like worker ants destroying anything they could, to the sounds of violent yells of hate and unleashed frustration. Broken furniture from the office was used to barricade the iron gate to our wing and more heavy objects were produced to reinforce it while the smashing and wrecking continued. In the dim light the angry contortions of the men's faces chilled me to the bone as we the prisoners tore down the prison that to us represented the oppression, anger and hate of all our years behind bars. We rampaged for our friends in other prisons who would love to have been here with us; we destroyed for all the people who had been released from prison; and we destroyed for those outside who the system had moulded and brainwashed and who would end up in prison as we had. And if there was any proof needed that long prison sentences did no good at all and only made people worse, well it was here, here in the men's faces and voices.

By now even the walls had been smashed so that you could pass from one cell to another, and in some places there were not even the remnants of a wall. When the action had begun classes were still in progress: the boys on classes had smashed what they could and then raided the canteen on their journey back to the wing. Before long the other wings had blown and prisoners were running everywhere, being helped over barricades to get into our wing. It was in every sense of the word a riot. The screws had taken up position far along the corridor leading to the yard; they had locked the gate behind them and were quite content to watch the proceedings from afar until such time as they were ordered to do otherwise. Gartree was now under the prisoners' control. The scene was like a battlefield, with rubble and wrecked debris everywhere. I myself tore about like a lunatic looking for anything that could be smashed. The whole of the main wing area had been completely wrecked in the space of twenty minutes. Then the cry went up for the small back room we used for a telly room, and which we had forgotten, to be smashed. Everyone charged to the back room screaming and shouting for it to be ripped to shreds. As the door was opened we all stood back to get a good view. Two prisoners were sitting facing each other playing poker, with their chips piled beside them. We were so amazed and shocked we just looked on opened-mouthed. They were both old boys and were well respected.

'George', I said, 'do you know there's a fucking riot going on with the whole bloody prison being torn down and you sit there calmly playing cards!'

'He's winning my money, Trevor, the old fox, he's been winning my money ever since we were kids and the first time I start winning some back everyone goes on the fucking rampage,' said George, calling his friend's bluff. Most of the time he spoke he kept his eyes keenly on the deck of cards, oblivious to the smashing-up of the room that was now under way.

'Leave the table for us, boys,' George said.

I was already on my way back to the centre of the wing where to my surprise I found four screws standing shaking, surrounded by prisoners and pleading to be let go. Some prisoners were talking about plunging them, killing them, doing them. Several of us intervened saying that they shouldn't be harmed because what we were reacting against was the abuse of prisoners by the doctor in particular and his medical staff; our aim was to get these points across, not to injure screws for the sake of it, which would in no way enhance our cause and would just give the prison authorities the opportunity to portray us as deranged psychopaths and schizophrenic animals who could only be calmed by drugs. It was decided to let the screws go and they were released over the barricade into the charge of their fellow screws, who by now were outside our gate in their hundreds. They obviously had a plan of sorts because the screws from our wing were at the front trying to be all nice and cordial to persuade us to take the barricade down, while the other screws, who must have been drafted in from nearby prisons, looked on.

It was hard to believe, but there was a phone working with an outside line and an orderly queue had formed to use it. 'Hello, mum, we're having a riot.' 'Don't bother coming down tomorrow, the whole place is smashed up.' Apart from conversations like that, we did also manage to get hold of the newsdesks of most of the daily newspapers and gave each of them an eyewitness account of what was actually happening and why it was happening. We kept them informed until we were finally cut off by the prison authorities.

The whole perimeter of the prison was now circled by police and army with guns, and a large squad of men dressed in black paramilitary garb with black helmets and visors, paratrooper's boots and round shields made of some sort of perspex had arrived. They stood in formation and ran in formation, and as they did so they banged their shields and let out incomprehensible war chants in an intimidating manner. It was not until the following year's disturbances at Wormwood Scrubs prison that the identity of this force became known. Called MUFTI (Minimum Use of Force Tactical Intervention), the squads had been secretly organised and trained in the aftermath of the 1976 Hull prison riot. There was not much that was minimal about the force they used.

The situation was obviously alien to our screws. Even though they had plans in case of a riot and knew how to deploy themselves and so on, they were still finding it hard to cope with the idea that their prison had been taken over by us. Through the gates and windows you could see that they were at a loss as to what to do with themselves as they milled about outside. It was now after nine o'clock and the MUFTI squad were preparing to charge the gate. I and four other prisoners were now on barricade duty. As the squad lined up along the passage the news was passed on, and our troops came from upstairs, downstairs, or wherever they were to reinforce the barricade. My heart beat faster and my whole body was drenched in sweat but I was not afraid – the stage for being frightened had long since passed. I was a soldier, a warrior protecting the fort from an enemy who I knew would threaten all our lives if they got past us. The MUFTI squad now took up their war chant and beat their shields in a crescendo of noise at the ready to charge. To combat this we prisoners took hold of any object that looked like it might make a good noise when banged and started up our own war chant. We were two sets of warriors facing up to each other: no quarter would be given and none asked. I surveyed our troops and saw their muscles highlighted, especially in the neck as our furious chant gathered volume. It was like a dream, it had to be a dream. I was in a war. No, we were in a war. How did I get here? What was I doing here? I was on top of the barricade, the front line, in the direct firing line, and it was too late to retreat even if I wanted to.

The faceless men clad in black began their advance slowly at first but picked up speed as they went along. I was screaming at the top of my voice, lost in darkness and a void of uncertainty. We had obviously anticipated attacks, in fact we knew it was inevitable, and we had drawn up plans of our own to combat any storming of our barricade. The iron gate which our barricade was built against consisted of a metal frame, with about six bars going from top to bottom leaving spaces between the bars wide enough to stretch your hand through and collect something on the other side from a friend – so anything that wasn't too big could be thrown through. The gate was about the shape and size of any household door, which meant there wasn't room for more than two people to approach it at once, and the fact that the passage started to slope upwards about five feet from the gate meant that anybody approaching had to walk uphill before reaching the gate. It was this that our battle plan rested on. The MUFTI squad's charge gathered momentum and as they neared the gate we put our plan into action. The countless gallons of liquid soap that were stored for the use of prisoners cleaning the wing were now produced and poured onto the slope leading up to the wing gate. The advancing MUFTI began falling and sliding into their comrades, who in turn fell like dominoes. It was like some slapstick comedy movie. Those who by chance managed to hang onto the bars were dealt with in the appropriate way. Some people were handing buckets to those on the barricade containing excrement of the vilest kind to be hurled at the advancing MUFTI, which surely would be enough to put off the most persistent. Stage two of our plan consisted of hot water from the urn which was situated right next to the gate – it gave a whole new meaning to the words 'steaming in'.

The attack was repelled as quickly as it started and we cheered and chanted our war cry at our obvious victory as the MUFTI scurried away to regroup and rethink their strategy. Our plan had been a resounding success. The expected second attack from the MUFTI never materialised. Instead came the pow-wow: some suited and booted bigwigs accompanied by screws came to talk to us. These men were undoubtedly very high up in the prison hierarchy and maybe even had come from the Home Office. By this time we had noticed several flashes going off and knew that journalists and photographers had also arrived, along with some prisoners' relatives. Their presence coincided with a change of strategy, hence the suited men arriving to talk to us. We were in charge, fully in charge, and it was our show. Before any of the men could talk we told them of our demands – not requests but demands. We told them we were not prepared to negotiate until our first demand had been met and that was the release of Yardy from the hospital. The sight of Yardy being physically carried by two inmates incensed the prisoners to fever pitch. Our demented war chant started up again and we even began smashing up things that had already been smashed, such was our fury. He was helped over the barricade by a hundred caring hands as the prison officers made themselves scarce.

It's difficult to describe emotions to people when talking about a situation that you yourself are personally involved in, but if I tell you that at the sight of Yardy I had to wipe water from my cheeks maybe you will understand how emotional I felt at the sight of him, helpless as a baby. He didn't know where he was, could not speak coherently and most certainly could not walk. There was no doubt in anybody's mind that he was drugged and any misgivings some may have felt about being involved in the riot were quickly dispelled by the sight of Yardy's obvious painful suffering. As he lay on a mattress, mouth agape and emitting gurgling sounds, it was obvious he was in a bad way.

Throughout the night of the riot we had contact with the other wings by runners passing to and fro, unmolested by the screws who at times vacated the passage to us, so we knew that the other wings were in virtually the same position as ourselves. As I surveyed the wing in the light of early morning I was surprised at the extent of the damage. It was as if a bomb had hit the place – the only thing missing was the smoke curling up from the debris into the air. Then began another round of talks, this time with Home Office officials, to whom we handed a list of our demands. Top of the list was the removal of a certain doctor from the prison. By the time we had reached point ten, I believe we had got into some real bullshit, like asking for the canteen to open longer – a demand put in by some funny guy. Since it was our wing that had started the riot the prison authorities concentrated most of their energies on trying to get our barricade down first, as they believed the others would then follow suit. The MUFTI were now outside in the yard and we could see them waiting, itching to have another go at getting in to crack heads, but they knew as well as we did that if they did manage to get in there would be serious injuries in the full flare of publicity. All the national newspapers were present and we were already front page news.

The prison authorities' tactics seemed to be to play a waiting game, and every so often they'd send a delegation to tell us we wouldn't be harmed, and that our personal property would in no way be smashed or tampered with if we took down the barrier. Of course they were met with howls of derision. But they were getting to some of the troops, who now began saying that we had achieved our objective of bringing media attention to the liquid cosh; others stated that as the prison was now a wreck, we'd done as much as we could this time and might as well live to fight another day; another group of people simply said they were hungry. Most of us knew in all seriousness that the time was drawing near when the barricade would have to come down. The prison had been wrecked and untold damage done, and the anger, frustration and hate which had led to the fury and frenzy of the previous night had now been satisfied. With the daylight came the realisation of what we had done, and we felt proud of it. At the same time some of us were like small boys with their hands behind their backs, making an arch with their feet in the dust and rubble, heads hung low as if to say, did I do this? They knew that they would be punished, and it seemed they would rather be punished now and get it all over and done with as quickly as possible. That evening it was decided to take the barricades down.

Yardy had by now recovered enough to sit up and talk. He still could not walk and complained of headaches, but at least he seemed to be on the road to recovery. Not one person believed that there wouldn't be reprisals by the hundreds of screws who now gathered at the entrances to all gates leading into the wings. If they didn't start here and now they would surely do so when we were inevitably moved to other prisons, where they would have welcoming parties ready to greet us as long lost friends and would show their affection for us by beating us about the head with their truncheons. Most of us retired upstairs when the barricade was about to be taken down and drew strength from one another. We were now all the same. Colour, creed, religion and size were all forgotten in our new-found equality, and the comradeship that flowed engulfed us all with a mutual respect. We knew that whenever we met again, be it inside or out, that respect would remain with us.

As the prison authorities came in to survey the damage, which they could only have guessed at up until this time, we the prisoners stood around or sat on whatever broken item could be found. I and a few others sat on broken piles of bricks while I played the guitar. As the prison delegation passed us someone else strummed the guitar to such wonderful melodies as 'We Shall Overcome', and 'We'll Keep the Red Flag Flying'. If I hadn't known already that I would be singled out for special treatment, I knew now: the look I was given by the suited men and the posse of screws left me in no doubt.

An hour after they had surveyed the damage they began the process of shipping us out to different prisons. The whole prison lay in ruins and we had to be put somewhere. It was like an army evacuation, with people hanging around waiting to be shipped out. It was a long drawn-out process, and none of us knew where we would end up. At three o'clock in the morning I was still awaiting my turn to be moved, along with several others. By this time we were both mentally and physically exhausted so there wasn't much talking, just apprehension about going out into the dark night on a journey into the unknown. My turn came about four in the morning and as I boarded the green barred van along with one other from my wing we were greeted with cheers by the prisoners left in the wings as they hung out of windowless windows. They cheered us as we had been cheering all day when other people had boarded the vans.

There were about seven prisoners from various wings on the van already and also several screws. I was very happy to note a black face hunched up in the corner of the van, but when I saw who it was, a nonce who had raped several girls, the happiness soon subsided and I sunk down into my seat. Like the others I was alone with my thoughts as the van pulled off to destination unknown. My mind again slipped into that light area of consciousness I had come to know so well during my years in prison.

I remember starting to think about how in the early seventies, amongst the afro hair do's and dashikis there was always that familiar call of 'Brother'. Those were the days that came soon after the Black Panthers, the days of Huey P. Newton, Bobby Seale, Eldridge Cleaver, Rap Brown, Angela Davis, the days when Curtis Mayfield was singing such classics as 'miss black America, and 'I'm from the other side of town', and Issac Hayes was to be continued. There was a feeling of oneness, a feeling of togetherness that embraced us as we began to realise who we were. Joined in mutual comradeship and happiness, we felt joy at finding ourselves, and what we shared with our brothers and sisters – the same predicaments, the same heartaches. We knew we weren't alone, and it was good to pass on the street without saying a word, smile, nod your head and say 'Brother' or 'Sister'. It was like a new dawn where everything kind of lit up. It was a happy time, if not so much in America, then, here it felt good to be young, gifted and black. People weren't ashamed to, 'say it loud, I'm black and I'm proud.' We got down and let our feelings out; we were at peace with ourselves; we had come of age and we loved ourselves and tried to take a pride in ourselves; we were people with dignity and pride. And Malcolm X said, 'We shall have our manhood by any means necessary,' and Bobby Seale said, 'Seize the time,' and

Angela Davis said, 'Brothers and sisters,' and George Jackson yelled, 'Freedom for all.' We young bloods screamed and stamped the floor in our happiness, as the old looked on and said 'Now don't you mix yourself up in that Black Power business.' Mohammed Ali denounced his slave name and Curtis Mayfield was still singing on, 'You're a winner', and 'You people who are darker than blue.' Wherever you went, you felt a part of something. Even though you probably couldn't explain it, you knew that it made you feel good not only with yourself but with others. You learnt to appreciate certain things in life, even if your life at the time wasn't all it might be. I know that everything wasn't rosy, but there was a true feeling of belonging and being in tune.

Of course, things don't go on forever and changes do occur, some for the worse and some for the better, but the burning passion of the late sixties and seventies has eluded us in the eighties. We seem to be in a decade of despair and no hope all the time searching for that pot of gold, fool's gold. In the sixties and seventies we had proud men and women to lead us on to better things, people in positions of power who lent a hand to those who weren't and called them 'Brother' and 'Sister'. They encouraged us and we in turn encouraged each other to reach greater heights. Curtis Mayfield was singing 'Move on up,' and when the music played it moved me. It showed me that I could one day be somebody who would command respect, simply and solely as a man.

We as black people have no control of the media, and therefore rely to a great extent on those black people who society says have 'made it'. We expect them, whether they like it or not, to give us information, show us the way, set standards. We expect those who are privileged, and who got where they are because we black people supported them, to stand up for us, but many of them have failed in the eighties. They have disowned us, they have lied, and worst of all they have cheated. They have taken our money and run. Many of them we have supported, turning up to live appearances in all kinds of weather buying records and books, going to stadiums and the cinema to support people who have given nothing in return. They line their own nests, then they jump on the merry-go-round of fantasy, where money and bleaching creams are the passports to disguise into the white world. I say to them, your time will come because you are traitors: not traitors in the field of black or white, because we're all human beings, but traitors because we sent you into the world to be a mouthpiece for us, to explain to people that we have certain needs; also to gain knowledge about the world and report back and let us know, because there are even things about ourselves we do not know and we might have hoped that you could find our for us. We have no media to explain our side of the story, yet you are there in the limelight and you say nothing.

Maybe one day those black superstars will have a decent thought and use their power. Weren't they even ashamed when a white man felt so bad about famine in Africa that he started doing something with his money, power, and influence? Too many of our superstars have sold out and are no more a part of us. Of course when questioned they offer some token gesture about being black, but it's usually more self-promotion than anything else. Million-dollar life-styles are fine if that's what they want, but they owe it to us to let the world know that we have real grievances that should be put right, because while they drink champagne, we still suffer. The stars of today who we should be looking up to are failing us, and you can see the results in the black community today.

The young are depressed and fed up because they have been led to believe everything hinges on money and if you don't have it you're a nobody. Well that's a lie. You can be what you want to be, you can be someone, you can be proud. But don't cheat yourself or others in the process. You don't have to use bleaching cream to succeed.

I vowed then that no matter where I went or what the future held they would never break me or my spirit. I thought again about the atrocities committed in South Africa, on my people in their own country, while the world stood back and watched as we were abused; I thought about the Aborigines and the Maori and how they were also abused; the Indians of America had virtually been wiped out; Third World countries had been raped, robbed and plundered – as I thought about all this the realisation came to me that people would one day rise up against those that had so wronged them with the abuse of their power. As the anger subsided my awareness took over, and with it came calmness and serenity. As a Somali guy had said to me, the truth cannot be hidden. He had said this as I ranted and raged like a madman, telling him that all our history had been hidden from us to the point where we had nothing to identify with. His words had so impressed me that even now they eased my mind, though at times I felt impatient for the truth to come out. I knew that in the end we would get it together and places like South Africa House, an affront to black people and to humanity, would be razed to the ground, because it was a symbol of oppression that was allowed to exist in the heart of a country that claimed to be a defender of truth and justice, because it represented all the lies ever told by the South African government. Yes, in time we would raze it to the ground ourselves, thank you. We would have our own hit squads and we'd assassinate South African presidents and diplomats who were allowed to come here free and unmolested. We'd breed our own Angela Davises, Malcolm Xs, George Jacksons, Huey P. Newtons, Eldridge Cleavers, Rap Browns . . . And we would learn to die! Yes, we would learn to die.

Chapter Nine

The van pulled up outside the gates of Lincoln prison and as we got out the number of screws that greeted us made us feel like real celebrities. So far there had not been any physical reprisals against us, but I must admit that at the sight of so many screws I actually thought our time had come. But we were all shepherded into the reception area and allocated cells in the block for what remained of the night and were left unmolested. I slept fully clothed with my boots on while sitting on the floor with my back against the door, in case they should try any of their tricks like steaming in when I was fast asleep. They wouldn't catch me that way.

Daylight had come and they were unlocking one by one for slop-out. It seemed that the block was empty but for our party. The governor, a man of about six foot, made his rounds and informed me it was his duty to tell me that I would be remaining in the block and would be charged with riotous acts committed at Gartree prison. With that he left. After ten minutes, through the hole in my spyhole cover, I could see the rest of the boys assembled ready to go on the wings. I heard a few of them ask for me, but they were told I would be staying in the block for the meantime and with that they were ushered out of the segregation unit. My dinner came and I was surprised at the quality of the food. Compared to what I was used to it was excellent. Two screws accompanied a prisoner as he wheeled a trolley with my food on it to the cell door and then left.

I had learned that Lincoln wasn't a long-term prison, nor was it maximum-security, and those here were doing fairly short sentences compared to my seven years, although where Lincoln was on the map I didn't have a clue. Half an hour before I was due to be unlocked to slop out, I heard the sound of footsteps outside my door, not the footsteps of people passing but of people congregating outside. I was immediately on full alert. I had already judged this prison to be somewhat easier going than any maximum-security prison, because when you're locked in the block in maximum-security prisons you are never allowed to keep your boots as I had done. The boots at least made me feel a bit more prepared for the trouble that was coming my way. My spyhole was raised and an eye looked through at me. 'You black bastard, you coon,' said the eye, as feet began kicking at my door and the sound of laughter echoed in my ears.

I knew the psychology behind what they were doing. It was quite obvious that they were baiting me, but I believed they wouldn't come in. They were winding me up, having their fun. The way they talked and the things they said led me to believe they were filth; they weren't even close to men because deep down they were cowards who were probably more afraid of me than I of them. They would have loved to have come in but they thought of the danger. Obviously by now they knew who I was and all about my record of assaults, and even though there were quite a few of them I was sure they understood that if they did come in at least one of them would not get out unscarred. That is why they stooped to the level they knew best – that of cowardice, using racial jibes to taunt me while hiding behind the locked door for protection. All their jibing and taunting was their way of testing me to see what calibre of man I was, and had I been found lacking in the way I dealt with the situation, then if not then and there but maybe on another occasion they would steam in and beat me badly. Their minds were unable to comprehend anything other than the superficial sterotyping – that was all they knew because they hadn't endeavoured to find out any more. To me this was understandable because the system hadn't trained them to deal with subjects like me. The system saw me as black and the only thing added to that was my number, so that was how they saw me too. Had I jumped up and begun ranting and raving I would only have reinforced the stereotype, and perhaps left myself wanting and lacking which could prove to be painful. Had I done nothing that would have been taken to be submissive, which I felt would also leave me wanting.

From the chair where I sat facing the wall I crossed the floor to within a foot of the door, looked directly at the eye in the hole and very coldly and calmly said, 'I know who you are and when this door is opened I'm gonna break your jaw,' putting emphasis on the last three words, and with that I sat down again facing the wall. Of course I hadn't a clue whose eye was at the hole, and anyway I think most of them outside had taken turns in poking their eye in and abusing me. To me it didn't matter. What I was going to do when the door opened I didn't know, but one thing I knew for sure was that I definitely would do something. It must have been quite confusing for them to have me issue such a statement in such a bold cockney accent as any villain would have done, and I'm sure it threw their stereotype into disarray because seconds later they had stopped. As I sat down and waited for the door to be unlocked, I began to reflect: was I a black villain? Had the system shaped me into that mould in the now four-and-a-half years I had been inside? I considered myself to be more versatile than that label suggested. I was able to get on with my black friends on one level, while also being able to make the transition when dealing with white friends – a kind of dual personality. The more I thought about it the more I could see the same trait in a few of my friends. We had been in a good few years now and we had fully learned the ins and outs of prison etiquette, not only learned them but adhered to them – things like never talking to a screw unless necessary, not letting anyone take liberties, looking after your own, black or white. Because we were staunch we mixed with people who were also of a staunch mould, people whom society would point a finger at and say, YES! Those men are villains. Firms sent messages to us and we to them. We had a comradeship, we were a clique, and as far as we were concerned it was them, the screws, and us. A lot of the prejudice and brainwashing that had been thrown on us, both black and white, by society had gradually been eroded away, leaving only men. I suppose it was something akin to being at war: it didn't matter who the man next to you was as long as he performed, that was all. A black face didn't mean shit if he wasn't staunch, and the same went for the white guys. The only criterion we had to judge by in prison was whether you were staunch or not.

If the average member of society could have seen me in this environment I suppose that yes, they would have labelled me a villain. I sat on the chair facing the wall, a kind of resigned fixed stare in my eyes. There was no room for compromise, my armour was on and I was ready to do battle. Why should I be so stubborn? Was it the need to prove myself? Why couldn't I just let it go? Suppose they killed me? What would happen if they tried drugging me? Couldn't I just forget the whole thing? No one else had heard them call me names, I could just pretend they hadn't said anything; but I couldn't I had heard, and they knew I had heard. It wasn't that I was stubborn or that there was any need to prove myself, but once you set a certain standard for yourself it's very difficult to live with yourself if you drop below it. I knew I was going to be in trouble and by my own standard and that of the system I was powerless to stop it. Taunts and names may be only words, but words are hurtful, people cry because of words, even if physical violence doesn't affect them. Words are very powerful – the names you call me show what you take me to be, and that's what matters. Because of my situation you think I'll accept it, I thought to myself. As far as you're concerned I'm in a no-win situation, but my forefathers are watching me, my family and friends are watching me, my girlfriend is watching, babies are watching, everybody is watching me, urging, pleading with me not to accept it. I know it's the normal practice, I know you've all done it lots of times before, I know everybody knows the game called stereotype and I know most people play it, but I don't and whenever you see me I want you to know I don't play that game because it's *your* game in which you made the rules so that you always win, and every time you play that game people get hurt inside and their souls weep. It affects them as human beings, as people, it's an insult and it will lead you to believe you can do with me what you will. Well I don't play that game!

As the door opened I gathered my plate to slop out. About eight screws stood outside my door, mostly with arms folded, but they couldn't disguise the apprehension on their faces and bodies and it made me feel good to see it. As I surveyed them I knew they weren't the heavies of the prison but merely opportunists. I made one trip to the recess and was on my way back to get fresh water in my jug when I saw the PO, the governor of these men, smirking and I knew I was going to do him. On the way back I carried the jug in my left hand and as I passed him I punched him full in the face with my right hand. Immediately his posse were on me. They dragged me kicking, spitting and cursing back to my cell where I banged and kicked my door, shouting a lot of vile filth: 'Come on, you shits, you want to make one, well come on. Please come in, please come in,' I hollered. 'Please, I want to die, please come and die with me, please.'

I was left alone and untroubled all day without any other meal. Nobody came near my cell until about seven o'clock, when an eye poked through the spyhole for a few seconds and disappeared, presumably to report back. What he saw when he looked in was a man preparing for war, because I knew they'd be back but this time they'd send the heavies. I was stripped to my underpants and boots, sweating profusely and doing rapid press-ups; and to add a nice touch, the second I heard the spyhole touched every press-up I did was accompanied by a warlike cry, just to let the watcher know I was prepared for whatever was to come. I was a madman.

They came about nine o'clock. Although they tried to muffle the sound of their footsteps as they approached my cell door, I still heard them. The door flew open and a sea of blue uniforms swamped me, kicking, punching, grabbing and trying hard to harm. Even though it may seem ludicrous, I did have a plan. As it was not possible to barricade myself into the cell, I decided I had two choices: the first was to accept whatever might happen to me, and the second was to fight. The first choice I dismissed immediately, but the second constituted somewhat of a problem – how could I fight off so many men with truncheons and God knows what else at their disposal when I had nothing? My mind was cleared of every kind of obstruction for the commencing battle. I forgot about the world outside, my family and friends, reinforcing the way I already thought – that I was totally on my own. If I died here then so be it. I believed it so much that I honestly thought I would never leave prison alive. It was like I was on a strange planet and could never get back to earth.

I was resigned for whatever was to come and planned to hold on to someone, anyone, and do as much damage as possible so that when they found me dead or whatever, at least they'd know who one of my attackers was. I had visions of them rolling me over in the morning and forcing my hands open still clutching someone's balls I had ripped off during the affray. As my war chant I selected Bob Marley's 'Slave Driver', and actually knelt down and prayed to my ancestors for strength to let me me acquit myself with honour so they would know that if they wanted to carry on with any more black people they had better be prepared. I actually felt happy! It was if my forefathers had lost the battle against slavery, but I was a new generation sent out into the wilderness to test my strength and courage. I promised myself not to be found wanting. Blows rained down on me from every angle. I was unable to see as I was swamped by the wave of blue, but at last I found it, an arm, a leg – a limb, anyway. I held on tight and sunk my teeth in; of the noise around me I was not conscious, but I heard that scream, that loud, piercing scream as I tasted blood and cloth: 'Ahhhhhh, get him off me, he's got my leg, ahhhhhh!' They played see-saw with the leg and me before finally backing off as I released his leg. They left carrying their wounded to the accompaniment of my war chant. I was a hero, even though nobody knew it except myself and those screws. I was proud of myself, I was happy, I had defended the honour of my people. So began another sleepless night as I kept vigil in case they returned; and every hour when the nightwatchman checked on me through the spyhole, he just found me training for war.

As soon as they slopped me out in the morning I threw everything out of my cell, ripped the shirt from my body and begged them to come back into my cell because I wanted to row. They didn't want to know. In the afternoon the governor and some medallion men assured me, for what it was worth, that I would be left alone and they would all bend over backwards, or it could have been forwards, to make sure I was OK. From that day it was if I had been given the freedom of the block. I could take showers every day, go to the library, and even say when I went on exercise. They said please and thank you, they did their best to keep me happy – but the price for all this was inevitably more remission lost.

Time carried on in much the same vein. Once they allowed me to go on the wing, but I was soon back in the block where I actually preferred to be, since I didn't fancy being regimented like some cabbage with the rest of them. At least in the block I could be alone with my thoughts. I never got bored. Most of the time I read or disciplined myself, for example by sitting on my chair all night without getting into my made-up bed, much to the amazement of the nightwatchman. Finally they delivered the charge sheets for my riotous acts at Gartree prison, which included possession of an offensive weapon, one table leg, inciting a riot, attempted physical assault on an officer with one table leg, handing out a box of Stanley knives to the rest of the prisoners, telling them to kill screws, starting a riot, and, believe it or not, mutiny. Where did they think we were, on *The Bounty* with Captain Bligh?

After about eight months they told me I would be leaving the next day to stand trial, and I could see the much-relieved look in the governor's eyes as he told me. Well, who could blame him? He must have been very happy to see me go after the way I had disrupted his prison. How could he forget the first time they let me up on the wing when I came down with the rest of the prisoners for tea and tipped over all the food because they claimed they didn't know I was on a Moslem diet and had nothing else to offer me apart from pork. Or the times I was placed on report and refused to see the governor, so he had to set up his table and adjudication board outside my closed cell door while I sang at the top of my voice. Or the time the woman from the Board of Visitors – who came round every month to ask if you had got any complaints but never did anything when you said you had – came to my cell and told the screw to open my door. The screw replied, 'Hercules doesn't want to see anybody.' That, in fact, *is* what I told them, but this persistent woman demanded that he open the door. The screw, bless his evil heart, began talking to me through the door, asking if it was all right if he opened the door, to which I replied, 'No.' He told me in a nervous sort of voice that he had to because this woman had demanded it. I agreed, only to be met with screams from the Board of Visitors woman, because as they opened the door there I was sitting on my chair stark naked having a wank and saying, 'Please do come in, madam, and make yourself at home.' Several years later I can still hear the scream as she fled from the cell.

Yes, all in all I think the governor was very pleased that I was leaving.

Chapter Ten

The hearing was a very quick and quiet affair. Most of us were tried locally, but I and a few others were picked out specially and brought back to London for trial. From Lincoln I went to Wandsworth and then moved on to the Scrubs. As usual, when I went into the hearing I told them I didn't believe in their system and whatever they chose to do or say was up to them, but for my part I would take no further part in any form or fashion. And that's exactly what I did. Throughout the proceedings I sat on a chair and looked straight ahead, and when I was spoken to I just ignored it. The reason I had come in the first place was because through the prison grapevine it had been agreed, much to my disgust, that people should go in but take no part. That I did, although left to my own devices I would not have even gone; I relented only to show solidarity with the others.

It was strange sitting in the room and hearing the accusations against myself. It was as if they were talking about someone else. It all seemed impersonal, as I suppose it would be when people are talking about you and referring to you and your mind is far away. Anyway, they carried on regardless and, surprise surprise, they found me guilty of all charges. There was one strange thing about the proceedings though, regarding my alleged attempted assault on a prison officer. After the screw had given evidence saying I had tried to hit him on the head while I was on barricade duty, another officer was called who was allegedly with this screw when I was supposed to have hit him. He was really a prosecution witness, but when he came in he claimed that as far as he was concerned he didn't see me do anything. I was almost tempted to talk and ask what the hell was going on, but I kept mute. Of course I was found guilty and relieved of 360 days remission, which is more or less the equivalent of two years because with remission you only do two-thirds of a sentence. Anyway, I was also sentenced to a few months in solitary; but since by this time I had already spent nearly a year in solitary it was really just a token gesture.

I still carry the scars of those many months of being on my own without seeing anybody. That long, lingering stare remains even to the extent that I don't even realise I'm doing it until I'm told. I have long bouts of quietness because one comes to realise that time goes on forever – sitting in a room with people without talking for twenty minutes is nothing to me, though it may seem a lot to others. I don't get lonely because now I am a loner. I've had to live with myself and know myself, and to analyse what I think and why and how, so I'm no stranger to myself. I know myself well, I've had to because at times I had no one else to turn to but myself. Yes, it leaves its scars. And even though one wouldn't wish to admit to it, after some time you do become an animal and how you see yourself is not how others see you. Even when you're released people see it in you, they feel it in you. You've crossed that boundary, or as they say, you've been there. I understand why they call it 'there' because to explain it is nigh on impossible. The only way you can relate it is to someone who's shared that experience, someone who's been there and knows what it's all about: hard men, hard life, and hard luck.

After my punishment was over I was transferred to Parkhurst on the Isle of Wight, which is said to be the end of the line, the last stop before Broadmoor. The trip over was a familiar journey and as I rode handcuffed in the van I reflected on the difference a few years can make. I now had no apprehension at all, because I knew what to expect. I was no more a green young man in the early flush of manhood who thought fighting and being bad was fun. I now knew it was a serious business and that life was a serious business; it was as if I had been to college, and in a sense my prison experience had been an education and I was now graduating. As the bus continued its climb up the steep hill leading to the summit where Parkhurst was situated, I couldn't help but think, you've been here before, son. And I didn't feel any fear or any nerves, my eyes were just fixed in a cold blank stare.

Parkhurst was little different. It was an institution where you were locked up just as in any other prison, and all the attitudes were much the same as I knew they would be. I had seen it all before. Yet I also saw that these attitudes reflected those of society outside, because the same men made the rules and they always made sure they won. But the tide was turning, however slowly it was definitely turning, and had somebody asked me then I could have told them that there are thousands, even millions, like me, who feel the same and will even act the same as I did. I know that many will have to travel the road I travelled to be able to understand and to put things into the right perspective.

Society as it stands now won't be able to stop the tide that is flowing, because if people believe that slavery, colonisation and imperialism will not extract a price then they are being naive. There are millions of people searching for their identity in an alien environment, they demand to find it and if they are not valued and respected for it then they rebel. You who could have learned from America but have chosen not to but instead to ignore the cry of a people who are lost and searching for themselves, you will pay the price. We don't want to be clones, absorbed into a white society, we want to be free to be ourselves.

And the time is running out.

Although Parkhurst was basically the same as the rest of the long-term prisons, there was one added quality that appealed to me and helped me settle down if not to a pleasant existence, then to one that at times bordered on the tranquil.

People sent to Parkhurst had usually been through the prison regime, 'seen it all before', moved from prison to prison until they finally ended up there. Others took a different route, in that they had been in prison before, been released and were now back. The authorities now deemed them real villains, beyond redemption and unlikely to put up with the bullshit and finickity annoyances of most of the other long-term prisons. This was a relief for me as the prisoners here were a bit older and more mature. In prison jargon, these were the real 'old lags'.

These older prisoners really ran the prison. They were laid back, more into giving advice than fighting. They were already established outside and inside, some even abroad; everybody knew their positions, and respect, believe me was paramount. There was no need for heavy stuff here, and no need for walking around with an inflated chest or a massive ego. I found and learned that the real villains rarely fought or argued or abused each other. But trouble could cost you your life, and not necessarily at the hands of the person you had the confrontation with. But the screws were hardly troubled and they themselves hardly troubled anyone, and this all lead to a much more tranquil existence within the boundaries of the prison walls. Of course yours truly still managed to get himself into trouble – not as bad as before, but trouble nevertheless. I realised, not for the first time, that part of the trouble was in me and with me: I was fighting for the right to be myself and at times it was not my outer self that was rebelling so much as my inner self, my soul crying. It was tormented, it was haunted, it craved for something else, it was not at peace with itself and continually disturbed me, forcing me to seek out the holy grail, which in my case was a black identity. It wanted me to speak a language I didn't know, a language long forgotten even by my forefathers, it wanted to get back to a land that it once upon a time remembered, it wanted to be in a place where it could hear my ancestors calling out to me.

Even when I had not been in prison my soul, my spirit, had cried out for its freedom, but now at least I understood that I was haunted because my spirit and soul were not free; and the first step to that freedom was to find my identity and become aware of who I was. My spirit showed me that my life might well be over, but that we all had a duty at least to show and explain to the young, those same youngsters who could end up in jail, dead, or whatever, without knowing who they were and without a chance to change their direction because of their ignorance.

While in Parkhurst an incident happened that brought the whole prison experience home to me and will live with me forever. Because of the delicate nature of the incident and its distasteful nature, I won't go into too much detail. On this day as usual we were unlocked to the hot-plate. As I was getting ready to come down to breakfast, one of the last as usual, I heard an almighty commotion and the alarm bells started ringing, accompanied by running feet and jangling keys. I knew immediately it was serious trouble – about what I didn't know, since there hadn't been any feuds I had been aware of and the prison was going through a relatively trouble-free period. I ran to the railings on my landing, as did several others both below and above, and there on the ground floor was a man lying in a pool of blood. No one said anything because if you had seen him you would have known he was dead. He was stabbed by another inmate who thought a liberty had been taken, but I'm sure if you asked the man who did it now he would put it down more to paranoia than to anything else.

That's how precarious life is in long-term institutions. At any time you could find yourself either dead or having killed someone, because the containment of human beings for many years in unnatural circumstances away from society only produces abnormal men who've lived so long in abnormal surroundings that they are incapable of normal judgment. These people will one day be back on the street and then society will have to cope with their distorted sense of what is right or wrong. The course our society is taking makes it blatantly obvious that our cities will end up like Detroit or New York, as life and liberty mean less and less. People are the products of their society, whether you wish to acknowledge that fact or not. Isolation and containment does not work, and no matter how many prisons are built they will be filled to capacity. Crimes will become more gruesome and bizarre, and anyone who thinks they're not safe now, well, hang around, society and its long-term prisons are moulding your worst nightmares.

Later in the morning after that unfortunate incident we went on exercise in the yard, and I remember myself and a few other black guys sitting on a wall and watching in amazement as the prison continued to function as if nothing had happened. The exercise yard was alive with activity as people continued their every day business. It was business as usual, and why not? After all, we lived with the ever-present threat of violence as a daily part of our lives, it was in us all, or the potential was in us all. Violence was not abnormal in our surroundings, and the ultimate (death) just around the corner. When it popped around to show us its face I suppose most people were not surprised; a lot probably knew that face very well, or at least it had flashed past them at some stage during their prison life.

But still the apparent normality of the exercise yard affected me and the people sitting on the wall deeply. One of the guys summed up the situation nicely: 'B-L-O-O-D C-L-A-R-T WE DIE IN A MADHOUSE'. And it really was a madhouse. Long-term prisons were madhouses, probably all prisons were madhouses, and the object for us was to come out sane.

Here we were, a man had been killed in an enclosed environment where everyone knew him, his life touched and related to every one of our lives, and yet questions such as whether we ourselves would actually leave here alive seemed totally irrelevant. Nobody was really analysing what had happened, how it came to happen, whether it could have been avoided what this really meant to us, where we went from here, and so on. No, people just carried on regardless. The most people wanted to know was 'Who got done?' and 'Who done him?' That was the extent of it. As long as it wasn't firm against firm and only two individuals, that seemed to make it a non-event, nothing to worry about, he's gone and that's it. We had been transformed into uncaring and unfeeling beings and most of us didn't even know it. We had come to accept what was abnormal to a vast society outside our prison walls as perfectly normal.

It made those of us sitting on the wall realise that prison was a very evil place, full of bad and dangerous people thrown into an evil institution to become even more bad and dangerous. We also realised that former prisoners' determination not to come back was such that they could and would do any form of wickedness to avoid this place; and that, we judged, would make them even more evil. It was a vicious circle, and let me tell you youngsters out there again that prison is a wicked and evil place and you'd better believe it.

If you see any alternative to the route to jail then I suggest you take it; but I also know from my experience that sometimes that's a lot easier said than done.

Time slid by in Parkhurst. I had nearly done my seven years, and I was told I would be released from prison in the next few weeks. As I laid down on my bed that night I began to think what it really meant to me.

When the assistant governor had called me into his office to tell me of my impending release, I sat quietly throughout his little speech. Most of what he said I didn't comprehend – not that I didn't understand his words, I just couldn't understand the idea of being released into the outside world. It was something alien to me. Other people were released, albeit very infrequently. I had long ceased to believe that I myself would one day be released – it was something one never thought about because it could quite easily destroy you.

In long-term institutions the subject of release really is a dark depressive cloud hanging over you. With people doing double-lives, thirty years recommended, even ten or twelve years, going around talking about your date of release was really frowned upon. It was always painful and distressing to others when someone else was leaving, since it brought the realisation that you would not be leaving for several years – and that was very disturbing mentally. In addition, uncertainty over parole and loss of remission meant that often people didn't even know their release date. No one counted their time in days, weeks or months but in years, and to dare dream of the outside would be to invite many sleepless nights and days that would seem endless. Most of all it would send you into a deep depression thinking of the years ahead of you.

As I lay down on my prison bed for the first time in several years, I allowed myself the luxury of letting my mind drift to the outside world and to the many things I had missed. I thought about women, their warm bodies and soft touch, and my whole body tingled with excitement at the prospect of making love to a woman – not tender, warm lovemaking, but hot, passionate, animal rutting, flesh on flesh and the slapping sounds of body against body with the sweet stench of sweat and the moans and groans of physical exertion as the climax is reached. It was as if those many years in prison needed to be released in a sexual frenzy.

But most of all I thought of what it would be like to be free of the confinement of an enclosed space, of being locked up in a small cell like an animal. I imagined what joy it would be to be away from the oppressive regime of prison, where we lived in such crushing proximity to each other, the same people day in and day out with no respite, the head-banging monotony and the claustrophobic tension that left you surviving on your nerve ends – these were the things I most looked forward to leaving behind.

Having started to think of what it would be like to be released, I then tried to block my mind to the rush of oncoming thoughts of freedom. But the seed had already been sown, and although I promised myself I wouldn't do it again and told myself I was not free and until such time that I was I would refrain from thinking of freedom, there still followed a very sleepless night.

I was released on a sunny day in October 1981, it was a quiet affair and quite an anticlimax, apart from a small emotional farewell when a few guys came to wish me luck. I had envisaged myself running around slagging off screws as I was leaving, but when the time came I didn't. In fact as I was leaving the screws looked quite pathetic. What kind of man would spend his days locking people up and taking their remission? It is like trading in human misery. I did allow myself one concession though: when I was going through the prison gates a screw said, 'Goodbye' to which I replied with my favourite words, 'Fuck off.' He seemed genuinely surprised and hurt – I don't know why because that same screw had placed me and my friends on report several times, telling the most incredible lies to get us in the block. It was as if the game was over and we should all shake hands and be friends; but as I've said on many occasions, I don't play that game.

I was given a holdall bag with shirts and trousers that looked like prison issue, a ticket for the ferry and twenty-five pounds. As I hadn't told anyone I was to be released, I didn't really have anywhere to stay, so I had been given a letter of introduction to a hostel in South London. As I stood at the bus-stop across the road from the prison, I stared at the gigantic and intimidating gates and wondered if my return was inevitable.

The wait at the bus-stop and the ride to the ferry were filled with selfconsciousness, not only because I seemed to be the only black person about, but also because I suspected that everybody knew I'd just been released from Parkhurst, what with my holdall bag, my ill-fitting clothes and my feeble attempts to suppress my desire to see everything at once with a wide-eyed stare.

It was the first time I had travelled inside a ferry as an ordinary passenger, but after a drink that left my head spinning and me grinning from ear to ear, I began to think how much I had changed in nearly seven years.

One thing I knew for sure, those seven years in prison hadn't done me any good at all – in fact quite the opposite. Prison doesn't help you to understand your crime or why you did it, nor does it help prepare you to go out into the world you left behind, the same world where you committed your crime. There was no form of reform, not even any attempt at it. If you were labelled a criminal and imprisoned, you would still be a criminal when you came out because there was nothing inside to dissuade you from criminality. When criminals are lumped together then criminality is accepted as quite normal, and nothing to be ashamed of. Prison is for confinement; or for spite – you've done something to society, so society will do something to you: jail, tit for tat.

Society is not interested in why so many people commit crimes, nor in delving into the ins and outs of it. Society doesn't care why they do it, doesn't care if it goes on forever. Even though of those who go to jail at least eighty per cent come back, society remains quite happy to play the merry-go-round game: you get out, you come back, you get out, you come back, and the more times you come back the more jails society will build.

Jail had made me more cynical, and the rough edges I had once had were now a hardened veneer. I knew for sure I would have difficulty in dealing with people or rather relating to them, because deep down within me I sensed a coldness that had not been there before coming to prison, a kind of cold detachment that could easily be switched on or off and not necessarily when I wanted.

I tried to see if I could think any positive thoughts about prison. I thought of how I had learnt to tolerate living in such confined spaces with others; but I realised that this tolerance was at the mercy of my moods and could easily turn, Jekyll-and-Hyde-like, into intolerance. And I realised that this Jekyll-and-Hyde personality must be a characteristic of most long-term prisoners.

So here I was on my way to a hostel in South London with twenty-five pounds in my pocket, with no idea of what to do with my life, no real prospects, and no one to turn to for help or advice. I was very much on my own. I had ceased writing to Dolly some time back, and I didn't know where my brothers and sisters were. I suppose I could have found out, but I felt this incredible aura about me, the stigma of a jailbird, and I thought it best not to burden them with it. 'Oh, by the way, this is my brother, he's just finished seven years in prison and been released from Parkhurst jail.' I could do without that, and the accompanying stares – indeed, I could do without any awkward questions about where I had been for the past few years. The elation I had first felt at being free was now tempered by the thought that perhaps I would return to criminal activity all over again. Most of my friends were what society called criminals – if not in the true sense of the word, then outcasts, rebels, people whom society frowned on and who in turn frowned upon society. Friends who believed we should tear down South Africa House, friends who believed we should bomb South African Airways, friends who believed the British government supported and conspired with South Africa. Friends who believed we needed to find our own black identity, friends who grieved and shed real tears of unhappiness over starvation in Africa and other places, knowing the governments of the world could alleviate the suffering almost overnight if they so wished, friends who knew that the economic and political turmoil in Africa and the Caribbean stemmed from slavery and colonialism. Friends who wanted to stand up and let their voices be heard about what they believed to be true, friends who wouldn't settle for mediocrity, who would find their own way in life and create a personal meaning to their lives, even if it meant opting out of the safe roles one could play within white society by becoming a clone of a white person – one could get through life easily with make-up and a smile like some clown, but that was the easy, soft option. Friends who thought how even more downtrodden (if that is at all possible) the people of South Africa would be had Nelson Mandela chosen the easy, soft option of conformity instead of speaking out loud and clear for what he believed, and then spending his life in jail for it.

The thought of returning to prison haunted me throughout my journey to London, but I did come to one decision: I would not compromise my beliefs, I would always stand up and be counted.

A small, Select Few who control the wealth of the world, the governments and the media are the people responsible for racism. Having sown the seeds of black inferiority, they happily sit back and watch as black people all over the world are subjected to humiliation and even death. The people who own the newspapers and television stations are allowed by the government, their friends, to write what they like about black people, while seldom portraying us on television in any kind of positive light. The Caribbean, for example, is always portrayed as a holiday resort for rich white people – lots of lovely sunshine, reggae music and steel bands with waiters serving cocktails, a real cool, lazy, laid-back place with black people shuffling around in straw hats with grinning white teeth, ready at anyone's beck and call to arrive with a glass of coconut rum punch, just like the adverts on television. Bullshit! People live in the Caribbean, work in the Caribbean, yet the only thing you see on television about the Caribbean is stereotyping us so that viewers have the impression that's all there is to black culture.

How many times have we as black people been out somewhere amongst white people who try to be polite in conversation by saying they've smoked weed or they like reggae music? That's all they know about black culture, because that's all they've ever seen or read about. In fact the great pyramids were built by black people who are now living in Nigeria. The original Egyptians were black, as the respected historian (white, I may add) Basil Davidson can confirm. Yet the media powers-that-be are quite happy for all Biblical characters to be white, unless of course they are slaves, and for all Egyptians to be white unless they are holding fans or are bodyguards with crossed arms, moody-looking faces and oily torsos. At the same time as depicting black people as white, the wealthy have greedily hoarded away black treasures of untold worth in museums across Europe – treasures which show that black people built the first civilisations on this planet. When we are ready, we'll want them back.

Our black past and history is gradually coming out of the shadows – bit by bit the truth is seeping through, the tip of the iceberg is showing through and black people can stand tall with pride and dignity.

Yet still Africa is portrayed as land of helpless people ravaged by famine and starvation, of witch doctors, half-naked women living in the bush as if that was all there was to Africa. The Select Few are happy for the TV and papers to show Africa in this light – it creates, albeit subconsciously, a feeling of superiority against helpless black people. When the first Europeans came to Africa, Africans had long since travelled to Europe and had occupied Spain for 600 years. The Portuguese explorer Vasco da Gama wrote in the early sixteenth century that Africa was a splendid and beautiful place, the people wore silk and they had beautiful buildings and a government that was superior to his own. What happened? What happened was that when raiders from France, Spain, England, Portugal, Germany and Holland came for our gold they destroyed all in their paths, burning, looting and killing.

They had things called guns which were beyond our belief and comprehension: how one could have a weapon that could kill a man at a hundred yards? What kind of evil was this? Our forefathers fled in terror as they were chased across the continent, running for their lives and those of their children, for even children were not safe from death.

The whole of Africa was in a terrible upheaval as more and more greedy and evil Europeans came to kill, plunder and trade on human flesh and suffering. African people could not defend themselves against the guns. They took to flight, leaving behind their homes, loved ones and way of life. Their very existence was under threat – mothers lost children, children lost mothers, killed or taken by force, and all lived in fear of white men. As they were on the run they lived in shelters that could be built quickly so they could leave at a moment's notice when white people came. They lived from the earth, eating what they could find at hand and wearing animal skins. They could not settle down to any form of stable life, and they lived in what Europeans referred to as 'mud huts' because their real homes had been destroyed.

After suffering hundreds of years being hounded like animals they then had to endure colonialism, when the Europeans came in force and carved Africa up, regardless of our own boundaries. They made laws alien to our people, took our wealth, treasure, minerals, gold, diamonds. They took our crops and exported them to their own countries and they got richer and richer as Africa become poorer and poorer. Colonialism was a form of slavery and to utter any word against the invaders was certain death.

While this was happening in Africa, the stolen slaves went to the West Indies, Britain, America, Portugal, Spain, South America – you name the place, black people were taken there in bondage. They weren't allowed to speak their language, they were branded, abused, hanged, whipped, burned in urns of boiling water. The law stated a slave was less than an animal – it wasn't against the law to kill a slave, he was your personal property to do with as you liked. We were not allowed to have relationships, children were sold on auction blocks, men were given to women and women to men as the masters decreed. Black people, slaves, built cities across America and Europe cities – Liverpool and Bristol, amongst numerous others in Britain, were built at the cost of black suffering and death.

Slaves in the West Indies and the Americas had to adapt to an alien way of life, their heritage and culture forgotten at the threat of a noose around their necks. When slavery was abolished black people everywhere had to endure a new kind of slavery – dependence, upon Europeans, on white men. Black people found themselves lost, in an alien environment, penniless and with nowhere to go. They were still regarded as slaves because the history of slavery was so ingrained into white culture that white people's attitudes hadn't changed. There was deep-rooted prejudice and violence towards an already suffering people, lost in an alien environment with nowhere to go. Still regarded as cheap labour, white men didn't wish to give any status to raise them from their lowly situation. A negro was still seen as an inferior animal, said not even to be human in the eyes of God: at one stage it was considered a crime for black people to believe in God.

Finding ourselves with nowhere to go our motherland Africa ravished and still controlled by Europeans, we were left in limbo, no man's land. We didn't know who we were or what we were, there was no meaning to life. While this was going on, Europe and America flourished at our expense. The world had changed and we as a black race hadn't changed with it, hadn't been allowed to change with it. In this new world we still found ourselves dependent on everyone for everything.

Our whole race had to find a direction, a meaning to life. We were always looked upon as inferior, a people without history, a people without a culture, a lost people in a lost land. While other peoples have been settled in their jealously-guarded lands for centuries, black people have to endure the knowledge that their lands were stolen from them, and in some cases still haven't been returned. How can we find our destiny when we're still in bondage, in slavery, in South Africa where the white minority still refuses to recognise us as equal human beings, still refuses to give us our land? What do we have to do? Do we have to kill before people will allow us to live as we wish and give us respect? You've taken all the gold and diamonds, for God's sake, what more do you want from us?

So when I go on a bus and don't want to pay, understand; when I don't want to work, understand; when I commit crimes, understand; when I don't give a fuck, understand;

when you show me in a bad light on TV and I come out of the house and say fuck you, understand; when you allow South African Airways to advertise on TV and I say fuck you, understand; while South Africa House stands in the West End, fuck you, fuck you, fuck you . . . One day we'll stop saying that, and that's when the trouble will begin. We as black people have been terribly wronged for thousands of years and we're still being wronged against, and *we all know it*, yet we are accused of being wrongdoers. You have stolen most of what we had, our birthrights, so that we black people scattered all over the world don't even know what tribe we belong to. We have no language or real culture, only that of being white clowns. Yet still you wish to oppress us because of our colour. Well, fuck you.

You went to America, killed off the Indians and stole their land; you went to Australia, killed off the Aborigines, who are black just like me, and stole their land and told us black people we couldn't go there if we so chose. You went to New Zealand, killed off the Maori people and stole their land. It seems the only people you go and kill and rob of their lands are *black people*. Well, fuck you.

Funny as it may seem, I see that this is not an issue between black and white but between the oppressors and the oppressed – but anyone who wants an insight into the anger and frustration of black people – well, now you know. No individual white person is to blame because there's good and bad in all, but these things have happened, albeit in the past, and cannot be forgotten. The Select Few who control the world and who happen to be white have had ample opportunity to right most wrongs, so that we human beings might coexist and live happily together on equal terms.

The fact that this Select Few are white has sometimes clouded the issue into black versus white and white versus black, but the real issue is that we all as human beings want to live in harmony with each other, our surroundings and nature. Why spend billions of pounds on nuclear weapons when people are hungry and thirsty and have nowhere to live, and countries are in state of near-collapse? The truth is that we, the human race, regardless of who we are, don't really want nuclear weapons. But the Select Few say we must have them. The world is being polluted, nature destroyed, but we don't want it this way. None of us want war, none of us want starvation in our world, none of us want racial hatred and conflict, none of us want our planet destroyed. Yet we live with these things or the threat of them. It is time to change, time to stand up for what we want, time to choose the leaders we want and spit out the Select Few who have set us on the road to ruin.

We can no longer close our eyes or pretend we don't know what's going on, because we do. We, humanity, can change life for the better. Each and every individual has a duty to this world, its children and all life on earth, to protect them and coexist in harmony and peace. This is not a pipe-dream, this can be a reality. If we want it, we can have it.